The Wellness Lifestyle

Comprehensive Approaches for Mind, Body, and Soul

Marlon Woolridge

The Wellness Lifestyle

*© Copyright 2024 by **Marlon Woolridge***

All rights reserved

This document is geared towards providing exact and reliable information with regards to the topic and issue covered. The publication is sold with the idea that the publisher is not required to render accounting, officially permitted, or otherwise, qualified services. If advice is necessary, legal or professional, a practiced individual in the profession should be ordered.

From a Declaration of Principles which was accepted and approved equally by a Committee of the American Bar Association and a Committee of Publishers and Associations.

In no way is it legal to reproduce, duplicate, or transmit any part of this document in either electronic means or in printed format. Recording of this publication is strictly prohibited and any storage of this document is not allowed unless with written permission from the publisher. All rights reserved.

The information provided herein is stated to be truthful and consistent, in that any liability, in terms of inattention or otherwise, by any usage or abuse of any policies, processes, or directions contained within is the solitary and utter responsibility of the recipient reader. Under no circumstances will any legal responsibility or blame be held against the publisher for any reparation, damages, or monetary loss due to the information herein, either directly or indirectly.

Respective authors own all copyrights not held by the publisher.

The information herein is offered for informational purposes solely, and is universal as so. The presentation of the information is without contract or any type of guarantee assurance.

The trademarks that are used are without any consent, and the publication of the trademark is without permission or backing by the trademark owner. All trademarks and brands within this book are for

clarifying purposes only and are owned by the owners themselves, not
affiliated with this document.

Table of Contents

Chapter 1: Mental Well-being and Emotional Resilience

Understanding Mental Health

Understanding mental health is fundamental to embracing a holistic wellness lifestyle. It's a journey of recognizing the intricate patterns of thoughts, emotions, and behaviors that shape our everyday experiences. Mental health is not merely the absence of mental illness; it is a comprehensive state of well-being where individuals realize their abilities, cope with normal stresses, work productively, and contribute to their communities.

The tapestry of mental health is woven with threads of biology, psychology, and social factors. Our genetic makeup predisposes us to certain mental health conditions, yet it's the interplay with our environment that often determines our psychological outcomes. Stressful life events, traumatic experiences, and constant exposure to negative environments can trigger or exacerbate mental health issues. Understanding these dynamics helps in fostering resilience and finding balance.

Resilience is the cornerstone of mental health. It is the mental reservoir of strength that people call on during difficult times, allowing them to manage stress and overcome adversity. Resilience involves behaviors, thoughts, and actions that can be learned and developed by anyone. It encompasses the ability to make realistic plans, maintain a positive self-view, communicate effectively, and manage strong feelings. Cultivating resilience requires a conscious effort to maintain flexibility and balance in life as one deals with stressful circumstances and traumatic events.

Emotional intelligence plays a pivotal role in mental well-being. It is the ability to recognize and understand one's own emotions and the emotions of others. This skill involves using emotional information to guide thinking and behavior, and managing emotions to adapt to different environments. People with high emotional intelligence are better equipped to handle interpersonal relationships judiciously and empathetically. Developing emotional intelligence involves self-awareness, self-regulation, motivation, empathy, and social skills, all of which contribute to emotional resilience.

Stress is an inevitable aspect of life, but chronic stress can have detrimental effects on mental health. It is essential to develop effective stress-reduction strategies to maintain mental well-being. Techniques like mindfulness meditation, deep breathing exercises, and progressive muscle relaxation can help in reducing stress levels. Mindfulness, in particular, encourages individuals to focus on the present moment, accepting it without judgment. This practice increases awareness and fosters a sense of calm and clarity, which can significantly alleviate stress.

The concept of a positive mindset is integral to mental health. It involves cultivating a mental attitude that focuses on the brighter side of life and anticipates positive outcomes. A positive mindset does not imply ignoring life's difficulties but rather approaching problems with a hopeful and constructive outlook. Techniques such as positive affirmations, gratitude journaling, and visualization can aid in fostering a positive mindset. These practices encourage individuals to focus on their strengths and achievements, helping them build resilience against setbacks.

Therapy and counseling are powerful tools for enhancing mental health. They provide a safe and supportive environment for individuals to explore their thoughts, feelings, and behaviors. Therapy can help people gain insights into their problems, develop coping mechanisms, and make positive changes in their lives. Different therapeutic approaches, such as cognitive-behavioral therapy, psychodynamic therapy, and humanistic therapy, cater to various needs and preferences. The therapeutic relationship, characterized by trust and collaboration, is central to the healing process.

Mental health is deeply interconnected with physical health. The mind-body connection implies that our mental state can influence physical health and vice versa. Regular physical activity, a balanced diet, and adequate sleep contribute significantly to mental well-being. Exercise, in particular, releases endorphins, the body's natural mood lifters, which can reduce stress and anxiety. Additionally, nourishing the body with a healthy diet rich in essential nutrients supports brain function and promotes mental clarity.

Social support is another crucial element in maintaining mental health. Humans are inherently social beings, and meaningful connections with others provide a sense of belonging and purpose. Positive relationships offer emotional support, reduce feelings of isolation, and increase resilience to stress. Building a strong support network involves nurturing relationships with family, friends, and community. It also entails reaching out for help when needed and being willing to offer support to others.

Spirituality and mental health often intersect, providing individuals with a sense of meaning and purpose. Spiritual practices can enhance mental well-being by promoting inner peace and connectedness. Whether through religious practices, meditation, or personal reflection, spirituality offers a pathway to understanding oneself and one's place in the world. It encourages individuals to explore their values, beliefs, and purpose, fostering a sense of fulfillment and contentment.

Mindfulness and meditation are powerful practices that enhance mental well-being by encouraging present-moment awareness. They involve focusing attention on the present, acknowledging thoughts and feelings without judgment. These practices have been shown to reduce symptoms of anxiety and depression, improve emotional regulation, and increase overall well-being. Incorporating mindfulness into daily life can involve simple activities like mindful eating, walking, or even breathing.

Mental health is a dynamic and evolving field, with ongoing research uncovering new insights into the mind. Advances in neuroscience, psychology, and psychiatry continue to shape our understanding of mental health, offering new avenues for treatment and prevention. Embracing mental health as an integral part of a holistic wellness lifestyle involves staying informed, seeking support when needed, and committing to personal growth and self-care.

Understanding mental health is not just an individual journey but a collective endeavor. It requires a shift in societal attitudes and perceptions, breaking down the stigma surrounding mental health issues. Education and awareness are key to fostering an environment where mental health is recognized as a vital component of overall well-being. By prioritizing mental health, individuals and communities can thrive, creating a world where everyone has the opportunity to live a fulfilling and balanced life.

Techniques for Enhancing Emotional Intelligence

Emotional intelligence is an essential aspect of well-being that influences how we navigate our personal and professional lives. It is the ability to recognize, understand, and manage our own emotions, as well as to recognize, understand, and influence the emotions of others. This skill is pivotal for building strong relationships, making sound decisions, and leading a fulfilling life. Developing emotional intelligence involves honing several key abilities: self-awareness, self-regulation, motivation, empathy, and social skills.

Self-awareness is the foundation of emotional intelligence. It involves recognizing one's own emotions and how they affect thoughts and behavior. Self-awareness requires introspection and mindfulness, allowing individuals to understand their emotional triggers and reactions. One effective technique for enhancing self-awareness is maintaining an emotional journal. By regularly documenting emotions and the circumstances that trigger them, individuals gain insights into patterns and can identify areas for growth. Reflecting on these entries fosters a deeper understanding of oneself and promotes emotional growth.

Self-regulation builds on self-awareness by enabling individuals to manage their emotions and impulses. This ability is crucial for maintaining balance and avoiding emotional outbursts. Techniques for self-regulation include practicing deep breathing exercises and mindfulness meditation, which help calm the mind and reduce stress. Another effective strategy is cognitive restructuring, which involves challenging negative thought patterns and replacing them with more positive and realistic ones. By practicing self-regulation, individuals can respond to situations with greater composure and clarity.

Motivation, another component of emotional intelligence, involves harnessing emotions to pursue goals with energy and persistence. It encompasses intrinsic motivation, which is driven by personal values and interests rather than external rewards. To enhance motivation, individuals can set clear, achievable goals and break them down into manageable steps. Visualizing success and celebrating small achievements along the way can boost motivation and reinforce a sense of accomplishment. Cultivating a growth mindset, where challenges are viewed as opportunities for learning and development, further fuels motivation.

Empathy is the ability to understand and share the feelings of others. It is a vital skill for building strong relationships and fostering compassion. Enhancing empathy involves active listening, where individuals fully engage with the speaker and seek to understand their perspective without judgment. Practicing empathy also requires being open to different viewpoints and experiences, which can be achieved by reading diverse literature, engaging in meaningful conversations, and volunteering in community service. By broadening one's perspective, individuals can develop a deeper connection with others and enhance their empathic abilities.

Social skills are the final component of emotional intelligence, encompassing the ability to manage relationships effectively.

These skills involve communication, conflict resolution, and collaboration. To improve social skills, individuals can practice assertive communication, where they express their needs and opinions clearly and respectfully. Role-playing different social scenarios can also help in developing effective communication strategies and building confidence. Additionally, learning to manage and resolve conflicts constructively is crucial for maintaining healthy relationships. This involves understanding different conflict styles, practicing active listening, and finding mutually beneficial solutions.

Mindfulness is a powerful technique that enhances all aspects of emotional intelligence. By cultivating present-moment awareness, mindfulness helps individuals become more attuned to their emotions and reactions. Regular mindfulness practice can improve self-awareness, self-regulation, and empathy, leading to more authentic and meaningful interactions. Simple mindfulness exercises, such as mindful breathing or body scans, can be incorporated into daily routines to promote emotional well-being and enhance emotional intelligence.

Emotional intelligence is not a fixed trait but a set of skills that can be developed and refined over time. It requires a commitment to self-improvement and a willingness to reflect on one's emotions and behaviors. By actively working on enhancing emotional intelligence, individuals can improve their relationships, communication, and overall quality of life. This journey of self-discovery and growth is a lifelong process, offering endless opportunities for learning and development.

The benefits of enhancing emotional intelligence extend beyond personal well-being to professional success. In the workplace, emotional intelligence is highly valued as it contributes to effective leadership, teamwork, and conflict resolution. Leaders with high emotional intelligence are better equipped to inspire and motivate their teams, creating a positive and productive work environment. They can navigate complex interpersonal dynamics and make informed decisions that consider the emotional impact on others. As organizations increasingly recognize the importance of emotional intelligence, it becomes a critical factor in career advancement and organizational success.

Enhancing emotional intelligence also contributes to mental and physical health. Individuals with high emotional intelligence are better able to manage stress and cope with life's challenges. They experience greater emotional resilience and are less likely to succumb to anxiety and depression. The mind-body connection is further strengthened as emotional intelligence promotes healthier lifestyle choices, such as regular exercise, balanced nutrition, and sufficient rest.

Building emotional intelligence is a transformative journey that requires dedication and practice. It involves a continuous cycle of learning, reflection, and growth. By embracing this journey, individuals can unlock their full potential and lead more fulfilling, connected, and meaningful lives. As emotional intelligence becomes an integral part of their identity, they cultivate a deeper understanding of themselves and others, enriching their relationships and enhancing their overall well-being.

In the pursuit of enhancing emotional intelligence, it is essential to approach the process with patience and compassion. Growth may not happen overnight, but with consistent effort and practice, individuals can make significant strides in their emotional development. Seeking support from mentors, coaches, or therapists can provide valuable guidance and encouragement along the way.

Ultimately, emotional intelligence is a powerful tool for living a balanced and fulfilling life. It empowers individuals to navigate the complexities of human emotions with grace and understanding, fostering a sense of harmony within themselves and their relationships. By prioritizing the development of emotional intelligence, individuals pave the way for a brighter, more empathetic, and connected world.

Building Resilience in Everyday Life

Resilience is an essential quality that empowers individuals to navigate the complexities of life with strength and optimism. It is the capacity to recover from setbacks, adapt well to change, and keep going in the face of adversity. In everyday life, resilience is not just about bouncing back from major life events; it's about maintaining balance and composure amid the daily challenges and stresses that everyone encounters. Cultivating resilience is a transformative journey that involves developing a set of skills and attitudes that bolster mental and emotional strength.

The first step in building resilience is fostering a positive outlook. Optimism is a powerful tool that shapes how individuals perceive and respond to life's challenges. It involves maintaining a hopeful and positive mindset, even when faced with difficulties. Instead of dwelling on problems, resilient individuals focus on solutions and opportunities for growth. They view setbacks as temporary and surmountable, which enables them to move forward with confidence. Cultivating optimism can be achieved through practices such as gratitude journaling, where individuals regularly note things they are thankful for, and by surrounding themselves with positive influences that uplift and inspire.

Another key aspect of resilience is developing strong problem-solving skills. Life is unpredictable, and challenges are inevitable. By honing problem-solving abilities, individuals can approach difficulties with a strategic mindset and find effective solutions. Problem-solving involves analyzing a situation, identifying possible courses of action, and evaluating their potential outcomes. It requires creativity, critical thinking, and the willingness to take calculated risks. Practicing problem-solving in everyday situations, such as resolving conflicts or managing time effectively, builds confidence and resilience.

Embracing change is also crucial for resilience. Change is a constant in life, and the ability to adapt to new circumstances is a hallmark of resilient individuals. Adaptability involves being open to new experiences, learning from change, and adjusting one's approach as needed. It requires flexibility and a willingness to let go of old habits or beliefs that no longer serve one's well-being. Developing adaptability can be nurtured by stepping outside one's comfort zone, seeking new challenges, and viewing change as an opportunity for growth and self-improvement.

Resilience is deeply rooted in self-awareness and self-care. Understanding one's emotions, strengths, and limitations is essential for managing stress and maintaining balance. Self-awareness enables individuals to recognize when they are feeling overwhelmed and to take proactive steps to address their needs. Practicing self-care involves prioritizing activities that nurture the body, mind, and soul, such as regular exercise, meditation, and spending time with loved ones. By taking care of themselves, individuals build the physical and emotional reserves needed to face life's challenges with resilience.

Social support is a critical component of resilience. Building and maintaining strong connections with family, friends, and community provides a valuable network of support during difficult times. These relationships offer emotional comfort, practical assistance, and a sense of belonging. By reaching out for help when needed and offering support to others, individuals strengthen their resilience and create a supportive environment that fosters well-being. Engaging in social activities, joining support groups, and participating in community events are ways to build and maintain a robust support network.

Another important element in building resilience is setting realistic goals and taking decisive action to achieve them. Goals provide direction and purpose, motivating individuals to persevere through challenges. Setting realistic and achievable goals involves breaking them down into smaller, manageable steps and celebrating progress along the way. By taking decisive action, individuals build momentum and confidence, reinforcing their resilience. Goal-setting also involves being flexible and willing to adjust one's approach if circumstances change or new information becomes available.

Mindfulness and meditation are potent practices that enhance resilience by promoting mental clarity and emotional stability. Mindfulness involves paying attention to the present moment with curiosity and acceptance, without judgment. By cultivating mindfulness, individuals become more aware of their thoughts and emotions, allowing them to respond to stress with greater calm and focus. Meditation, on the other hand, is a practice that encourages relaxation and introspection, helping individuals build inner peace and resilience. Incorporating mindfulness and meditation into daily routines can significantly enhance one's ability to cope with stress and adversity.

Lastly, resilience is strengthened by learning from past experiences. Reflecting on previous challenges and identifying the lessons learned helps individuals gain valuable insights and prepare for future difficulties. This process involves acknowledging both successes and failures, understanding what worked and what didn't, and using this knowledge to inform future decisions. By learning from the past, individuals build wisdom and resilience, equipping themselves to face new challenges with greater confidence and competence.

Building resilience is an ongoing journey that requires dedication and effort. It is a dynamic process that involves cultivating positive attitudes, developing practical skills, and nurturing supportive relationships. Resilience empowers individuals to navigate life's ups and downs with grace and fortitude, transforming challenges into opportunities for growth and self-discovery. By prioritizing resilience, individuals create a foundation for lasting well-being and fulfillment, enabling them to thrive in all areas of life.

Strategies for Stress Reduction

Stress, an unavoidable companion in the tapestry of life, often weaves its way into our daily experiences, impacting both our mental and physical well-being. Yet, understanding and implementing effective strategies for stress reduction can transform this often debilitating force into a manageable aspect of life. It requires identifying the roots of stress, understanding its manifestations, and actively engaging in practices that promote relaxation and resilience.

A crucial first step in managing stress is awareness. Recognizing stressors—those circumstances or situations that trigger stress responses—enables individuals to address them directly. These stressors can range from daily annoyances, like traffic jams and work deadlines, to significant life changes, such as moving house or changing jobs. Keeping a stress journal can help identify patterns and triggers, offering insight into how stress arises and providing a starting point for managing it effectively. By documenting emotions and reactions, individuals can gain clarity and begin to implement targeted strategies for stress reduction.

One of the most effective strategies for stress reduction is practicing mindfulness. Mindfulness is the art of paying attention to the present moment without judgment. This practice encourages an awareness of thoughts, feelings, and sensations, promoting a sense of calm and clarity. Techniques such as mindful breathing and body scan meditations can be incorporated into daily routines, providing a mental oasis amidst the chaos. These practices help anchor individuals in the present, reducing anxiety about the future and regrets about the past, fostering a peaceful state of mind.

Breathing exercises are another powerful tool in the stress-reduction toolkit. When faced with stress, our body's natural response is to enter a state of heightened alertness, often accompanied by shallow breathing. Deep breathing exercises counteract this response by activating the parasympathetic nervous system, which promotes relaxation. Techniques such as diaphragmatic breathing, where one inhales deeply through the nose, allowing the diaphragm to expand, and exhales slowly through the mouth, can be practiced anytime, anywhere. Regular practice of these techniques can lower heart rate, reduce blood pressure, and create a sense of tranquility.

Physical activity is a well-documented stress buster. Engaging in regular exercise releases endorphins, the body's natural mood elevators, which help counteract the effects of stress. Whether it's a brisk walk in the park, a yoga session, or a high-intensity workout, physical activity provides an outlet for pent-up energy and frustration. It also offers an opportunity to disconnect from stressors and focus on the rhythm and movement of the body, creating a meditative experience that calms the mind.

Another effective strategy for reducing stress is cultivating a supportive social network. Humans are inherently social creatures, and meaningful connections with others provide emotional support and a sense of belonging. Sharing one's concerns with trusted friends or family members can offer perspective, lighten emotional burdens, and reinforce that one is not alone in facing challenges. Engaging in social activities, volunteering, or joining community groups can also provide opportunities to connect with others and build supportive relationships.

Time management is an essential skill in reducing stress. Often, stress arises from feeling overwhelmed by responsibilities and tasks. Effective time management involves prioritizing tasks, setting realistic goals, and delegating when possible. Creating a structured schedule and breaking tasks into manageable steps can help alleviate feelings of being overwhelmed. Additionally, setting boundaries and learning to say no to additional commitments can prevent overloading oneself, allowing for a more balanced and stress-free life.

Incorporating relaxation techniques into daily life can significantly reduce stress levels. Practices such as progressive muscle relaxation and visualization help the body and mind transition from a state of tension to one of relaxation. Progressive muscle relaxation involves tensing and then slowly relaxing each muscle group in the body, promoting a state of physical relaxation. Visualization, on the other hand, involves imagining a peaceful scene or situation, allowing the mind to escape from stressors and find tranquility. Both techniques can be practiced in short sessions throughout the day, providing an immediate sense of relief.

A healthy lifestyle also plays a crucial role in managing stress. Nutrition, sleep, and hydration all impact the body's ability to cope with stress. Consuming a balanced diet rich in essential nutrients supports overall well-being and provides the energy needed to manage stress effectively. Adequate sleep is vital for physical and mental restoration, enhancing resilience to stress. Staying hydrated ensures that the body functions optimally, as even mild dehydration can exacerbate stress levels. By prioritizing these aspects of health, individuals can bolster their defenses against stress.

Engaging in hobbies and activities that bring joy and relaxation is another effective stress-reduction strategy. Whether it's painting, gardening, playing a musical instrument, or reading a book, dedicating time to activities that foster creativity and relaxation can provide a welcome respite from stressors. These activities offer an opportunity to engage in something enjoyable and fulfilling, promoting a sense of satisfaction and reducing stress.

Finally, seeking professional help when needed is a vital strategy for managing stress. Therapists and counselors can provide guidance, support, and coping strategies tailored to individual needs. They can help individuals explore the underlying causes of stress and develop personalized plans for managing it. Therapy offers a safe and confidential space to express concerns, gain insights, and work towards solutions.

Incorporating these strategies into daily life requires commitment and practice. It involves creating a personalized plan that aligns with one's lifestyle, preferences, and needs. By actively engaging in stress-reduction practices, individuals can build resilience, enhance their well-being, and transform stress from an overwhelming force into a manageable aspect of life. Through this journey, they cultivate a deeper understanding of themselves and develop the tools needed to thrive in the face of life's challenges.

Cultivating a Positive Mindset

Embracing a positive mindset is an art that transforms how individuals perceive and interact with the world. It is not about ignoring life's challenges but about approaching them with a constructive and hopeful attitude. Cultivating a positive mindset is an empowering practice, enabling people to navigate life's complexities with resilience and grace. This chapter delves into actionable strategies that foster positivity, enhance well-being, and unlock personal potential.

The journey toward a positive mindset begins with self-reflection. Understanding one's current thought patterns is crucial for identifying areas for growth. Negative thoughts often stem from ingrained beliefs or past experiences, shaping how individuals interpret situations. By taking time to reflect on these patterns, individuals can gain insight into how negativity manifests in their lives. Journaling is a powerful tool for self-reflection, allowing individuals to document their thoughts and identify recurring themes. This practice fosters self-awareness and sets the foundation for positive change.

Reframing negative thoughts is a transformative strategy for cultivating positivity. It involves consciously shifting perspective to view situations in a more optimistic light. For example, instead of viewing failure as a setback, individuals can reframe it as a learning opportunity. This shift from a fixed mindset to a growth mindset encourages people to see challenges as opportunities for development. By practicing reframing, individuals can break free from the cycle of negativity and embrace a more positive outlook.

Gratitude is a cornerstone of a positive mindset. It involves recognizing and appreciating the good in life, no matter how small. Practicing gratitude shifts focus from what is lacking to what is abundant, fostering a sense of contentment and fulfillment. Keeping a gratitude journal, where individuals regularly note things they are thankful for, can enhance this practice. Expressing gratitude to others, whether through a simple thank you or a heartfelt note, strengthens connections and reinforces positivity in relationships.

Visualization is another effective technique for fostering a positive mindset. By mentally picturing desired outcomes, individuals can motivate themselves and reinforce a sense of possibility. Visualization involves creating a vivid mental image of achieving goals, experiencing success, or overcoming challenges. This practice taps into the power of imagination, making positive outcomes feel more attainable and real. Regular visualization exercises can boost confidence, enhance motivation, and align actions with aspirations.

Surrounding oneself with positivity is vital for maintaining a positive mindset. The people, environments, and media individuals engage with influence their thoughts and emotions. By choosing to surround themselves with supportive and uplifting influences, individuals can reinforce positivity in their lives. This may involve spending time with encouraging friends, seeking out inspiring literature, or engaging in activities that bring joy and fulfillment. Creating a positive environment fosters an atmosphere of growth and optimism.

Mindfulness is a practice that enhances positivity by promoting present-moment awareness. It encourages individuals to observe their thoughts and emotions without judgment, fostering a sense of acceptance and peace. Mindfulness practices, such as meditation and mindful breathing, help quiet the mind and create space for positive thoughts to flourish. These practices can be integrated into daily routines, providing a mental sanctuary amidst life's hustle and bustle. By cultivating mindfulness, individuals can develop a deeper connection with themselves and the world around them.

Affirmations are powerful tools for reinforcing a positive mindset. These are positive statements that individuals repeat to themselves, often daily, to challenge and overcome negativity. Affirmations can be tailored to specific goals or areas of growth, such as self-confidence or resilience. By consistently repeating affirmations, individuals can rewire their thought patterns, making positivity a natural and automatic response. This practice builds self-belief and encourages individuals to embrace their potential.

Acts of kindness, both towards oneself and others, amplify positivity and create a ripple effect of goodwill. Simple gestures, such as offering a compliment, helping a neighbor, or volunteering, can boost mood and foster a sense of connection. Kindness towards oneself involves self-compassion, treating oneself with the same care and understanding as one would offer a friend. By practicing kindness, individuals can enhance their well-being and cultivate a community of positivity and support.

Embracing change is an essential aspect of a positive mindset. Life is dynamic, and the ability to adapt to new circumstances with an open heart is a hallmark of positivity. Instead of resisting change, individuals can view it as an opportunity for growth and exploration. This mindset requires flexibility and a willingness to embrace new experiences. By welcoming change, individuals can expand their horizons and discover new facets of themselves and the world.

Finding meaning and purpose in life contributes significantly to a positive mindset. Engaging in activities that align with one's values and passions fosters a sense of fulfillment and direction. This may involve pursuing a hobby, volunteering for a cause, or setting personal goals that reflect one's aspirations. By focusing on what truly matters, individuals can create a life rich with purpose and joy.

Lastly, celebrating progress, no matter how small, reinforces a positive mindset. Acknowledging achievements and milestones, whether personal or professional, boosts confidence and motivation. Celebrating progress involves recognizing effort, perseverance, and growth, rather than solely focusing on end results. By celebrating the journey, individuals can cultivate a sense of pride and accomplishment, fueling further positivity and success.

Cultivating a positive mindset is a lifelong journey of self-discovery and growth. It requires commitment, practice, and a willingness to embrace change. By implementing these strategies, individuals can transform their thought patterns, enhance their well-being, and lead a fulfilling life. Positivity becomes not just a mindset but a way of being, influencing every aspect of life and radiating outward to inspire others. Through this journey, individuals unlock their potential and create a world of possibilities and joy.

The Power of Therapy and Counseling

Therapy and counseling have long been recognized as powerful tools for personal growth and healing. They offer individuals a safe space to explore their thoughts, emotions, and experiences, providing insight and guidance on the journey toward self-discovery and well-being. Engaging in therapy or counseling is not a sign of weakness; rather, it is a courageous step toward understanding oneself better and fostering emotional resilience.

At its core, therapy is about creating a supportive and non-judgmental environment where individuals can openly express their feelings and explore their innermost thoughts. This process is facilitated by trained professionals who provide empathy, insight, and expertise to help individuals navigate the complexities of their lives. Whether facing specific challenges or seeking personal development, therapy offers a structured approach to addressing issues and achieving goals.

One of the most significant benefits of therapy is the opportunity for self-reflection. In the hustle and bustle of daily life, it is easy to become disconnected from one's emotions and needs. Therapy provides a dedicated time and space to pause, reflect, and gain clarity. Through guided exploration, individuals can uncover patterns of behavior, identify emotional triggers, and understand the underlying causes of their feelings. This self-awareness is a crucial step in personal growth, enabling individuals to make informed decisions and create meaningful change.

Therapy also plays a vital role in building coping skills and resilience. Life is filled with challenges, and the ability to navigate these with grace and fortitude is essential for well-being. Therapists equip individuals with practical tools and strategies to manage stress, regulate emotions, and cope with adversity. These skills empower individuals to face life's ups and downs with confidence, fostering a sense of control and stability.

Another powerful aspect of therapy is its ability to heal past wounds. Many individuals carry unresolved trauma or painful experiences that shape their thoughts and behaviors. Therapy provides a safe and supportive environment to process these experiences, release pent-up emotions, and find closure. By working through past traumas, individuals can break free from the hold of negative patterns and create a healthier, more fulfilling future.

Therapy also enhances interpersonal relationships. Understanding oneself better naturally extends to understanding others more deeply. Through therapy, individuals learn effective communication skills, empathy, and conflict resolution strategies that improve their interactions with others. Whether in personal or professional relationships, these skills foster stronger connections, reduce misunderstandings, and build trust.

For those dealing with mental health challenges, therapy is an invaluable resource. Conditions such as anxiety, depression, or post-traumatic stress disorder can be overwhelming and debilitating. Therapists provide evidence-based interventions and support to help individuals manage symptoms and improve their quality of life. Cognitive-behavioral therapy, for example, focuses on identifying and changing negative thought patterns, while mindfulness-based approaches promote present-moment awareness and relaxation.

Moreover, therapy encourages personal empowerment and self-acceptance. It challenges individuals to confront self-limiting beliefs, embrace their strengths, and recognize their inherent worth. This process of empowerment enables individuals to take ownership of their lives, set boundaries, and pursue their goals with confidence. As individuals learn to accept themselves fully, they cultivate a deep sense of self-love and compassion.

The therapeutic journey is a deeply personal one, with various approaches and modalities to suit individual needs and preferences. Some may benefit from traditional talk therapy, while others find solace in art therapy, music therapy, or other creative expressions. Group therapy offers a sense of community and shared experience, while individual therapy provides personalized attention and support. The key is finding the right fit, where individuals feel comfortable and supported in their healing journey.

While therapy provides numerous benefits, it's essential to approach the process with an open mind and realistic expectations. Personal growth is a gradual process that requires patience and commitment. Progress may not always be linear, and challenges may arise along the way. However, with persistence and dedication, therapy can lead to profound transformation and healing.

The power of therapy and counseling lies in their ability to facilitate change from within. They empower individuals to explore their inner worlds, confront challenges, and embrace their potential. Through this transformative process, individuals can create a life that aligns with their values, aspirations, and true selves.

For those considering therapy, it's important to remember that seeking help is a courageous and positive step. It is an investment in oneself, offering the opportunity for growth, healing, and a more fulfilling life. By engaging in therapy, individuals embark on a journey of self-discovery that can lead to lasting change and empowerment.

As the journey unfolds, individuals may find that the skills and insights gained through therapy extend beyond the therapy room, enriching all aspects of life. They may experience greater emotional resilience, improved relationships, and a deeper sense of purpose and fulfillment. Therapy becomes not just a tool for healing but a lifelong resource for growth and self-awareness.

In a world where mental health is increasingly recognized as a vital component of overall well-being, therapy and counseling stand as pillars of support and transformation. They offer individuals the chance to explore their inner landscapes, confront challenges, and create a life that reflects their true selves. Through this journey, individuals unlock their potential, embrace their strengths, and cultivate a life of authenticity and joy.

Chapter 2: Physical Health and Vitality

The Essentials of a Balanced Diet

A balanced diet is a fundamental cornerstone of health and well-being, influencing everything from physical vitality to mental clarity. It provides the body with essential nutrients required for energy production, cellular repair, and overall maintenance. Understanding and implementing the principles of a balanced diet can lead to improved health outcomes, enhanced performance, and a greater sense of overall well-being.

At its core, a balanced diet is about variety and moderation. It incorporates a wide range of foods to ensure the intake of essential nutrients, including carbohydrates, proteins, fats, vitamins, and minerals. These nutrients serve as the building blocks of the body, each playing a unique role in maintaining health. A diet that emphasizes diversity not only meets nutritional needs but also adds enjoyment and flavor to meals.

Carbohydrates are the body's primary energy source, fueling everyday activities from walking to thinking. Not all carbohydrates are created equal, however. Complex carbohydrates, found in whole grains, legumes, and vegetables, provide sustained energy and are rich in fiber, which aids digestion and promotes satiety. Simple carbohydrates, such as those found in sugary snacks and drinks, should be consumed in moderation, as they can lead to energy spikes and crashes. By prioritizing complex carbohydrates, individuals can maintain stable energy levels and support overall health.

Proteins are essential for growth, repair, and the production of enzymes and hormones. They are composed of amino acids, some of which the body cannot produce on its own and must be obtained from the diet. Lean meats, fish, eggs, dairy products, legumes, and nuts are excellent sources of protein. Incorporating a variety of protein sources ensures a complete intake of essential amino acids and supports muscle health, immune function, and tissue repair.

Fats, often misunderstood, are a vital component of a balanced diet. They serve as a concentrated energy source, aid in the absorption of fat-soluble vitamins, and support cell structure and function. Unsaturated fats, found in foods like avocados, nuts, seeds, and olive oil, are considered heart-healthy and can help reduce inflammation. Saturated fats, present in animal products and certain oils, should be consumed in moderation. Trans fats, often found in processed and fried foods, should be avoided due to their negative impact on heart health. By choosing healthy fats, individuals can enjoy their benefits while minimizing risks.

Vitamins and minerals are micronutrients that play crucial roles in numerous bodily functions. They support immune health, bone strength, and energy metabolism, among other things. A diet rich in fruits, vegetables, whole grains, and lean proteins typically provides a sufficient supply of these nutrients. Each color of fruit and vegetable represents different vitamins and minerals, so "eating the rainbow" ensures a comprehensive intake. For some individuals, such as those with dietary restrictions or specific health conditions, supplements may be necessary to meet their nutritional needs, but these should be taken under the guidance of a healthcare professional.

Hydration is an often-overlooked aspect of a balanced diet. Water is essential for maintaining body temperature, transporting nutrients, and removing waste. It acts as a lubricant for joints and aids in digestion. Daily water needs can vary based on factors such as age, gender, activity level, and climate, but a general guideline is to drink at least eight 8-ounce glasses of water a day. Consuming foods with high water content, such as fruits and vegetables, also contributes to hydration. Proper hydration supports overall health and can enhance physical and cognitive performance.

Mindful eating is a practice that complements a balanced diet by fostering a healthy relationship with food. It involves paying attention to hunger and fullness cues, savoring flavors and textures, and eating with intention. Mindful eating encourages individuals to listen to their bodies and make choices that satisfy both nutritional needs and personal preferences. This approach can prevent overeating, reduce stress, and promote a more enjoyable eating experience.

Meal planning is a practical strategy that supports a balanced diet. By planning meals in advance, individuals can ensure a variety of foods, control portion sizes, and reduce reliance on processed or convenience foods. Meal planning also helps manage time and budget constraints, allowing for more intentional and healthful eating. Preparing meals at home, using fresh ingredients, provides greater control over nutritional content and can be a creative and rewarding endeavor.

Cultural and personal preferences play a significant role in shaping dietary choices. A balanced diet can be adapted to fit different lifestyles, traditions, and tastes. Whether following a vegetarian, vegan, Mediterranean, or other dietary pattern, the principles of balance, variety, and moderation remain key. By respecting personal and cultural preferences, individuals can create a sustainable and enjoyable eating plan that supports long-term health.

While a balanced diet is a powerful tool for promoting health, it is important to recognize that individual needs can vary. Factors such as age, gender, activity level, and health status can influence nutritional requirements. Consulting with a registered dietitian or healthcare professional can provide personalized guidance and ensure that dietary choices align with individual health goals and needs.

Incorporating the essentials of a balanced diet into daily life is a lifelong journey that evolves with changing needs, preferences, and circumstances. It is about making informed choices, enjoying a variety of foods, and nourishing the body and mind. Through this journey, individuals can cultivate a deeper understanding of nutrition and its impact on well-being, empowering them to lead vibrant and healthful lives.

Exercise and Its Role in Wellness3 Understanding

Exercise is a vital component of overall wellness, serving as a catalyst for both physical and mental health. It transcends the mere act of movement, embodying a lifestyle that promotes longevity, vitality, and emotional balance. Understanding the role of exercise in wellness involves exploring its multifaceted benefits, integrating physical activity into daily routines, and fostering a mindset that values self-care and personal growth.

Physical activity is a powerful antidote to the sedentary lifestyle that has become increasingly prevalent in modern society. It combats the negative effects of prolonged inactivity, which can lead to a myriad of health issues such as obesity, cardiovascular disease, and metabolic disorders. Regular exercise boosts cardiovascular health by improving circulation, reducing blood pressure, and enhancing heart function. It strengthens muscles and bones, increases flexibility, and promotes balance and coordination, reducing the risk of injury and improving overall quality of life.

The benefits of exercise extend far beyond the physical realm, profoundly impacting mental health and emotional well-being. Physical activity is a natural mood enhancer, stimulating the production of endorphins—hormones that create feelings of happiness and euphoria. This natural high can alleviate symptoms of anxiety and depression, providing a healthy outlet for stress relief. Exercise also improves sleep quality, enhancing energy levels and cognitive function during waking hours.

Incorporating exercise into daily life requires a thoughtful approach that aligns with individual goals, interests, and abilities. The key is finding activities that are enjoyable and sustainable, transforming exercise from a chore into a rewarding experience. Variety is essential to maintaining motivation and preventing burnout. Whether it's a brisk walk in the park, a yoga session, a dance class, or a weightlifting routine, the options are vast and cater to diverse preferences.

For beginners, starting with moderate-intensity exercises, such as walking or cycling, can ease the transition into a more active lifestyle. These activities are accessible, require minimal equipment, and can be easily integrated into daily routines. As confidence and fitness levels improve, individuals may choose to explore more vigorous forms of exercise, such as running, swimming, or high-intensity interval training (HIIT). The gradual progression helps prevent injury and ensures long-term adherence to an active lifestyle.

Strength training is a crucial component of a balanced fitness regimen, offering benefits that complement cardiovascular exercise. It involves using resistance to build muscle strength and endurance, contributing to a toned physique and improved metabolic rate. Strength training can be accomplished through various means, including free weights, resistance bands, or body-weight exercises like push-ups and squats. Incorporating strength training into a fitness routine enhances muscle mass, supports bone health, and aids in weight management.

Flexibility and balance exercises are equally important, as they enhance mobility and reduce the risk of falls, particularly as one ages. Activities such as yoga, Pilates, and tai chi focus on stretching and controlled movements, promoting flexibility and core stability. These practices also encourage mindfulness and relaxation, further contributing to emotional well-being.

The social aspect of exercise should not be underestimated. Engaging in group activities or team sports fosters a sense of community and connection, providing motivation and accountability. Whether it's joining a local running club, participating in group fitness classes, or organizing friendly games with friends, the camaraderie and shared goals enhance the exercise experience.

Setting realistic goals is vital for maintaining motivation and tracking progress. Goals should be specific, measurable, achievable, relevant, and time-bound (SMART), providing a clear framework for success. Whether the aim is to run a 5K race, improve flexibility, or simply increase daily activity levels, setting and achieving goals fosters a sense of accomplishment and reinforces a commitment to wellness.

Listening to one's body is paramount in any exercise regimen. It's important to recognize the difference between pushing through discomfort and risking injury. Rest and recovery are integral to the exercise process, allowing the body to heal and adapt to increased physical demands. Adequate hydration, nutrition, and sleep also support recovery and enhance performance.

Exercise should be viewed as an ongoing journey rather than a destination. It evolves with changing needs, preferences, and circumstances, adapting to different life stages and challenges. Embracing this dynamic nature allows individuals to remain engaged and committed to their wellness journey, continually reaping the benefits of an active lifestyle.

For those facing barriers to exercise, such as time constraints, physical limitations, or lack of motivation, finding creative solutions is key. Short bursts of activity, such as taking the stairs instead of the elevator or engaging in a quick home workout, can make a significant difference. Technology, in the form of fitness apps or online classes, provides convenient and accessible ways to stay active.

Ultimately, the role of exercise in wellness is profound and far-reaching. It empowers individuals to take charge of their health, enhancing physical and mental resilience. By embracing a lifestyle that values movement and self-care, individuals can unlock their full potential and enjoy a life of vitality and balance. Through the journey of incorporating exercise into daily life, individuals discover the transformative power of movement and its ability to enrich every aspect of their well-being.

the Body's Signals

The human body is a remarkable organism, constantly communicating through an intricate language of signals and cues. Understanding these signals is pivotal for maintaining health and well-being, as they offer invaluable insights into the body's needs, conditions, and potential issues. This chapter delves into the art of listening to the body, interpreting its language, and responding with care and intuition.

Every sensation, from hunger pangs to muscle soreness, is a message from the body, indicating its current state. Hunger is perhaps the most familiar signal, typically arising as a result of the body's need for energy and nutrients. However, it's important to differentiate between true hunger and cravings triggered by emotional or environmental factors. True hunger manifests gradually, often accompanied by physical sensations such as stomach growling or light-headedness, whereas cravings tend to be sudden and specific, usually linked to emotional states or habits. By tuning into these subtle differences, individuals can make informed decisions about their dietary intake, ensuring they nourish their bodies appropriately.

Thirst is another critical signal that demands attention. Often mistaken for hunger, thirst indicates the body's need for hydration. Dehydration can lead to a host of issues, including fatigue, headaches, and impaired cognitive function. Recognizing the signs of thirst, such as dry mouth, dark urine, or a decrease in energy levels, is essential in maintaining optimal hydration. Regular water intake throughout the day, rather than waiting for thirst to occur, supports overall health and bodily functions.

Pain serves as a protective mechanism, alerting individuals to potential harm or injury. It is the body's way of signaling that something is amiss, prompting immediate attention and action. Acute pain, resulting from injury or inflammation, is typically sharp and intense, urging individuals to rest and recover. Chronic pain, on the other hand, persists over time and may indicate underlying conditions requiring medical intervention. By acknowledging and addressing pain signals, individuals can prevent further damage and promote healing.

Fatigue is a common signal indicating the need for rest and recuperation. While occasional tiredness is normal, persistent fatigue may signal underlying health issues or lifestyle imbalances. Factors such as inadequate sleep, poor nutrition, stress, and lack of physical activity can contribute to feelings of exhaustion. By identifying the root causes of fatigue and making necessary lifestyle adjustments, individuals can restore their energy levels and enhance overall well-being.

The body also communicates through its response to stress. In moments of stress, the body activates the "fight or flight" response, releasing hormones such as adrenaline and cortisol. While this response is essential for handling immediate threats, chronic stress can have detrimental effects on health. Symptoms such as increased heart rate, shallow breathing, and muscle tension are indicators that the body is under stress. Implementing stress-reduction techniques, such as deep breathing, meditation, or physical activity, can help calm the nervous system and restore balance.

Digestion offers a wealth of signals about the state of one's health. The process of digestion is a complex interaction of multiple systems, and any disruption can manifest as bloating, gas, or discomfort. These signals can indicate food intolerances, dietary imbalances, or stress-related digestive issues. Paying attention to digestion and making dietary changes, such as increasing fiber intake or managing stress, can alleviate discomfort and promote gastrointestinal health.

The skin, the body's largest organ, provides visible signals about internal health. Changes in skin condition, such as dryness, rashes, or discoloration, can reflect nutritional deficiencies, allergies, or underlying medical conditions. Monitoring skin health and addressing any changes with appropriate skincare or dietary modifications can enhance both appearance and overall health.

Sleep patterns are another important indicator of health. Regular, restful sleep is essential for physical and mental restoration. Disruptions in sleep, such as insomnia or frequent waking, can signal stress, anxiety, or lifestyle factors that require attention. Establishing a consistent sleep routine, creating a restful environment, and addressing stressors can improve sleep quality and overall well-being.

Listening to the body involves a holistic approach, integrating physical, emotional, and mental awareness. It requires mindfulness and attentiveness, creating space for self-reflection and introspection. Practicing mindfulness techniques, such as meditation or yoga, fosters a deeper connection with the body and enhances the ability to interpret its signals accurately.

Cultivating this awareness is an ongoing journey, requiring patience and practice. It involves learning to trust one's intuition and understanding that the body is a reliable guide. By honoring its signals and responding with compassion and care, individuals can maintain a harmonious balance between mind, body, and spirit.

Understanding the body's signals is akin to learning a new language, one that can profoundly impact health and well-being. By becoming fluent in this language, individuals can make informed choices that support their health, prevent illness, and promote a sense of vitality and balance. This journey of self-discovery and awareness empowers individuals to take charge of their health, fostering a deeper connection with the body and a greater appreciation for its wisdom. Through this process, the body becomes not just a vessel, but a trusted ally in the pursuit of a vibrant and fulfilling life.

Importance of Sleep and Recovery

The importance of sleep and recovery in maintaining optimal health cannot be overstated. In a world that often glorifies busyness and productivity, sleep is sometimes relegated to the sidelines, viewed as an expendable luxury rather than a fundamental necessity. However, sleep is a critical component of the body's restorative processes, influencing physical health, cognitive function, and emotional well-being. Understanding the profound impact of sleep and recovery is essential for cultivating a balanced and healthy lifestyle.

Sleep serves as a vital mechanism for the body's repair and rejuvenation. During sleep, the body undergoes various restorative processes, from cellular repair to hormone regulation. It is during this time that the brain consolidates memories, processes emotions, and clears out toxins accumulated during waking hours. Adequate sleep enhances cognitive performance, improving attention, problem-solving abilities, and creativity. Conversely, sleep deprivation can lead to cognitive impairments, affecting decision-making, reaction times, and overall mental clarity.

The physical benefits of sleep are equally significant. Quality sleep supports immune function, reducing the risk of infections and illnesses. It plays a role in regulating metabolism and body weight, as hormonal imbalances caused by inadequate sleep can lead to increased appetite and weight gain. Sleep also contributes to cardiovascular health, with studies showing that poor sleep patterns are linked to an increased risk of heart disease, hypertension, and stroke. By prioritizing sleep, individuals can enhance their physical health and reduce the risk of chronic conditions.

Emotional well-being is intricately linked to sleep quality. Sufficient rest promotes emotional regulation, helping individuals manage stress, anxiety, and mood fluctuations. Sleep deprivation, on the other hand, can exacerbate feelings of irritability, sadness, and anxiety, impacting personal and professional relationships. By fostering a consistent sleep routine, individuals can nurture their emotional resilience and maintain a positive outlook on life.

Establishing healthy sleep habits is crucial for achieving restorative sleep. A consistent sleep schedule, where individuals go to bed and wake up at the same time each day, helps regulate the body's internal clock. Creating a sleep-conducive environment, free from noise, light, and distractions, supports relaxation and improves sleep quality. Limiting exposure to screens and electronic devices before bedtime is also important, as the blue light emitted can interfere with the production of melatonin, a hormone that regulates sleep.

The role of recovery extends beyond sleep, encompassing activities that support physical and mental restoration. Active recovery, such as gentle stretching, yoga, or walking, promotes blood circulation and muscle relaxation, aiding in the recovery process. Passive recovery, which includes rest days or relaxation techniques like meditation and deep breathing, allows the body to recuperate without added stress. Balancing active and passive recovery is essential for preventing overtraining and burnout, particularly for those engaged in regular physical activity.

Nutrition plays a supportive role in sleep and recovery. Consuming a balanced diet rich in nutrients such as magnesium, potassium, and tryptophan can promote relaxation and improve sleep quality. Foods like bananas, almonds, and turkey are known to contain these sleep-enhancing nutrients. Hydration is equally important, as dehydration can lead to discomfort and disrupt sleep. Avoiding caffeine and heavy meals close to bedtime can prevent sleep disturbances and enhance the recovery process.

Stress management is a critical aspect of optimizing sleep and recovery. Chronic stress activates the body's stress response, releasing hormones such as cortisol that can disrupt sleep patterns. Incorporating stress-reduction techniques, such as mindfulness meditation, progressive muscle relaxation, or journaling, can help calm the mind and prepare the body for restful sleep. By addressing stressors and implementing relaxation practices, individuals can create a more harmonious sleep environment.

The interplay between exercise and sleep is another important consideration. Regular physical activity has been shown to improve sleep quality, increase sleep duration, and reduce the time it takes to fall asleep. However, the timing and intensity of exercise can influence sleep patterns. Engaging in vigorous exercise close to bedtime may energize the body and delay sleep onset. Instead, scheduling workouts earlier in the day or opting for calming activities in the evening can promote better sleep.

Listening to the body's signals is essential for balancing sleep and recovery needs. Recognizing signs of fatigue, such as daytime sleepiness, difficulty concentrating, or mood changes, indicates the need for rest and recuperation. Honoring these signals and allowing the body to rest when needed supports overall health and well-being. It is important to approach sleep and recovery with a mindset of self-compassion, understanding that rest is not a sign of weakness but a vital component of self-care.

The societal perception of sleep as a non-essential activity is slowly shifting, with growing recognition of its importance for health and productivity. Emphasizing the value of sleep in workplace and educational settings can lead to improved performance, reduced absenteeism, and enhanced overall well-being. Encouraging flexible schedules, providing opportunities for rest, and promoting a culture that values wellness can create environments where individuals thrive.

Sleep and recovery are foundational to a balanced and healthy life, influencing every aspect of well-being. By prioritizing restorative sleep, embracing recovery practices, and cultivating healthy habits, individuals can unlock their full potential and enjoy a life of vitality and resilience. This holistic approach to health recognizes the interconnectedness of mind, body, and spirit, fostering a deeper appreciation for the restorative power of rest. In this journey towards wellness, sleep emerges not as an afterthought but as a cornerstone of thriving in an ever-demanding world.

Preventative Health Practices

Preventative health practices are the cornerstone of a proactive approach to wellness. By taking steps to maintain health and prevent disease, individuals can lead longer, healthier lives and reduce the burden of chronic illnesses. These practices encompass a range of activities and lifestyle choices, each contributing to overall health and vitality.

Nutrition plays a pivotal role in preventative health. A balanced diet, rich in fruits, vegetables, whole grains, and lean proteins, provides the necessary nutrients to support bodily functions and prevent nutrient deficiencies. Antioxidants found in colorful fruits and vegetables protect cells from damage, reducing the risk of chronic diseases such as cancer and heart disease. Omega-3 fatty acids, present in fish and flaxseeds, promote heart health and reduce inflammation. By prioritizing nutrient-dense foods and minimizing processed foods high in sugar, salt, and unhealthy fats, individuals can significantly lower their risk of developing lifestyle-related diseases.

Physical activity is another essential component of preventative health. Regular exercise strengthens the heart, improves circulation, and helps maintain a healthy weight. It lowers the risk of developing conditions such as hypertension, diabetes, and certain cancers. Exercise also enhances mental health by releasing endorphins, the body's natural mood elevators. Engaging in a mix of aerobic, strength, flexibility, and balance exercises ensures a comprehensive fitness routine that supports all aspects of health. Even small changes, like taking the stairs instead of the elevator or going for a short walk during lunch breaks, can have a positive impact on health.

Routine health screenings and check-ups are vital for early detection and prevention of diseases. Regular medical exams, such as blood pressure checks, cholesterol tests, and cancer screenings, help identify potential health issues before they become serious. Vaccinations are another critical preventative measure, protecting individuals from infectious diseases and their complications. Staying up-to-date with recommended vaccines not only safeguards personal health but also contributes to community immunity, protecting those who are vulnerable or unable to receive certain vaccines.

Stress management is crucial for maintaining both physical and mental health. Chronic stress can lead to a host of health problems, including heart disease, depression, and weakened immune function. Techniques such as mindfulness meditation, deep breathing exercises, and yoga promote relaxation and help manage stress levels. Taking time to engage in hobbies, connect with loved ones, and pursue activities that bring joy and fulfillment can also alleviate stress and enhance overall well-being.

Adequate sleep and recovery are fundamental to preventative health. Sleep is a restorative process that allows the body to repair and rejuvenate. Lack of sleep is linked to a range of health issues, including obesity, diabetes, and impaired cognitive function. Establishing a regular sleep routine, creating a calming sleep environment, and addressing sleep disturbances can improve sleep quality and support overall health.

Hydration is often overlooked but is essential for maintaining health. Water is vital for digestion, nutrient absorption, temperature regulation, and joint lubrication. Dehydration can lead to fatigue, headaches, and impaired concentration. Drinking an adequate amount of water each day, and adjusting intake based on activity level and climate, supports the body's functions and promotes vitality.

Social connections and community involvement are powerful determinants of health. Strong social ties provide emotional support, reduce stress, and promote a sense of belonging. Engaging in community activities, volunteering, or joining clubs and groups can foster meaningful relationships and improve mental health. These connections are particularly important as people age, helping to combat loneliness and isolation.

Avoiding harmful behaviors is a key aspect of preventative health. Smoking, excessive alcohol consumption, and drug use can have serious health consequences. Smoking is a leading cause of preventable death, linked to lung cancer, heart disease, and respiratory illnesses. Resources and support groups are available for those seeking to quit smoking or reduce alcohol consumption, providing guidance and encouragement throughout the process.

Environmental factors also play a role in preventative health. Minimizing exposure to pollutants, chemicals, and toxins can reduce the risk of respiratory ailments, allergies, and other health issues. Simple actions, such as using natural cleaning products, ensuring proper ventilation, and reducing plastic use, contribute to a healthier environment and personal well-being.

Education and awareness empower individuals to make informed choices about their health. Staying informed about health and wellness topics, understanding risk factors, and recognizing the signs and symptoms of potential health issues enable individuals to take charge of their health. Accessing reliable health information from reputable sources, participating in health education programs, and consulting with healthcare professionals provide the knowledge needed to make proactive health decisions.

Preventative health practices are not a one-size-fits-all approach; they require personalization and adaptation to individual needs and circumstances. Cultural, genetic, and lifestyle factors influence health, and recognizing these differences allows for tailored strategies that best support individual wellness goals. By embracing a holistic approach to health, individuals can integrate preventative practices into their daily lives, fostering a sense of empowerment and control over their well-being.

The journey towards preventative health is a continuous process of growth, adaptation, and learning. It is about making conscious choices that prioritize health and embracing a lifestyle that supports longevity and quality of life. By committing to preventative health practices, individuals invest in their future, laying the foundation for a life of vitality, resilience, and fulfillment. This proactive approach to health not only enhances personal well-being but also sets a positive example for others, contributing to a healthier and more vibrant community.

Integrating Movement into Daily Life

Integrating movement into daily life is a transformative approach to health and well-being, offering a dynamic alternative to traditional exercise routines. In an era where sedentary lifestyles have become the norm, finding creative ways to incorporate physical activity throughout the day can bring significant benefits to both physical and mental health. By embracing a lifestyle that values movement, individuals can enhance their vitality and improve overall quality of life, all while navigating the demands of modern living.

The human body is designed for movement, yet many aspects of contemporary life discourage it. From long hours spent at desks to the convenience of vehicles and technology, inactivity often prevails. This lack of movement can contribute to a host of health issues, including obesity, cardiovascular disease, and muscular imbalances. To counteract these effects, it's essential to integrate movement into daily routines, making it an effortless and enjoyable part of life rather than a task to be scheduled.

One of the simplest ways to incorporate more movement is by rethinking the commute. Walking or cycling to work not only increases daily activity levels but also provides an opportunity to enjoy fresh air and reduce stress. For those with longer commutes, parking farther from the destination or getting off public transport a stop early can add valuable steps to the day.

These small changes accumulate over time, significantly boosting physical activity.

The workplace presents unique challenges for staying active, yet it also offers opportunities for creativity. Standing desks or adjustable workstations encourage movement and reduce the health risks associated with prolonged sitting. Taking short, frequent breaks to stretch or walk around the office can invigorate the mind and body, enhancing productivity and focus. Organizing walking meetings or incorporating brief exercise sessions into the workday fosters a culture of wellness and keeps energy levels high.

At home, daily chores become opportunities for movement. Activities such as gardening, cleaning, or home repairs require physical effort and can be as beneficial as a gym workout. Engaging in these tasks with mindfulness and enthusiasm not only improves the home environment but also contributes to personal fitness. Dance parties in the living room, playing with pets, or enjoying active games with family members turn leisure time into moments of joyful movement.

Social gatherings can be reimagined to include physical activity. Instead of meeting friends for coffee or dinner, consider planning active outings such as hiking, bowling, or playing a sport together. These activities strengthen social bonds while promoting health and well-being. Community classes or group fitness events offer opportunities to try new activities and connect with others who share similar interests in an active lifestyle.

Technology, often blamed for encouraging sedentary behavior, can also be harnessed to promote movement. Fitness apps and wearable devices track activity levels, set goals, and provide reminders to move. Online workout classes and video tutorials make it easy to explore new forms of exercise from the comfort of home. Virtual challenges or competitions with friends can add motivation and accountability, turning movement into a fun and engaging pursuit.

Integrating movement into daily life also involves a shift in mindset. Viewing movement as a source of joy and vitality rather than a chore fosters a positive attitude toward physical activity. Celebrating small victories, such as reaching a step goal or mastering a new yoga pose, reinforces the habit of movement and builds confidence. By focusing on the pleasurable aspects of movement, individuals can sustain their commitment to an active lifestyle.

Mindfulness plays a crucial role in this transformation. Being present and attentive during movement enhances the experience and deepens the connection with the body. Whether it's feeling the rhythm of the breath during a walk or the stretch of muscles in a yoga pose, mindfulness enriches the practice of movement and cultivates a sense of gratitude for the body's capabilities.

Incorporating movement into daily life does not require drastic changes or a complete overhaul of existing routines. Instead, it involves small, incremental adjustments that align with personal preferences and lifestyle. The key is to identify opportunities for movement that resonate with individual interests and make them an integral part of everyday life.

The benefits of this approach extend beyond physical health. Movement stimulates the release of endorphins, lifting mood and reducing stress. It enhances cognitive function, improving memory and concentration. By fostering a sense of accomplishment and empowerment, movement boosts self-esteem and emotional resilience.

Ultimately, the integration of movement into daily life is a journey of self-discovery and empowerment. It is about reclaiming the joy of movement and recognizing its potential to transform health and well-being. By making movement a natural and enjoyable part of life, individuals can unlock a world of vitality and fulfillment, embracing each day with renewed energy and enthusiasm. Through this approach, movement becomes not just an activity but a way of life, enriching every moment and inspiring a lifelong commitment to health and happiness

Chapter 3: Nourishing the Soul

Exploring Spiritual Practices

Spiritual practices have long been a cornerstone of human culture, offering pathways to inner peace, personal growth, and a sense of connection to something greater than oneself. In a world often fraught with stress and uncertainty, these practices provide solace and guidance, anchoring individuals in a deeper understanding of life's purpose. Whether rooted in religious tradition or secular exploration, spiritual practices invite introspection, compassion, and a commitment to personal and collective well-being.

At the heart of many spiritual practices is the pursuit of mindfulness—a state of being fully present and engaged with the current moment. Mindfulness invites individuals to observe their thoughts and feelings without judgment, fostering a sense of clarity and peace. Practices such as meditation, deep breathing, and mindful movement encourage this heightened awareness, offering a refuge from the distractions and demands of everyday life. By cultivating mindfulness, individuals can develop a deeper appreciation for the present moment and a more compassionate relationship with themselves and others.

Meditation, a practice with roots in ancient traditions, remains a powerful tool for spiritual exploration. It involves quieting the mind and focusing attention, often through techniques such as breath awareness, visualization, or mantra repetition. Meditation offers a sanctuary from the noise of the external world, providing space for reflection and self-discovery. Regular meditation practice has been shown to reduce stress, enhance emotional resilience, and improve overall well-being. For beginners, starting with just a few minutes a day can lay the foundation for a transformative practice.

Prayer is another spiritual practice that transcends cultural and religious boundaries. It serves as a form of communication with the divine, offering individuals a way to express gratitude, seek guidance, or find comfort. Prayer can be formal or informal, structured or spontaneous, and often reflects personal beliefs and values. It provides a sense of connection to a higher power and reinforces a sense of purpose and meaning in life. For many, prayer is a source of strength and inspiration, guiding them through life's challenges and triumphs.

Journaling is a reflective practice that allows individuals to explore their inner world through the written word. It involves capturing thoughts, emotions, and experiences on paper, creating a tangible record of personal growth and understanding. Journaling can be a form of self-expression, a tool for problem-solving, or a means of processing complex emotions. By engaging in regular journaling, individuals can gain insights into their beliefs, values, and aspirations, fostering a deeper connection to their spiritual journey.

Rituals and ceremonies are integral to many spiritual traditions, providing structure and meaning to significant life events and transitions. Whether celebrating a birth, honoring a marriage, or mourning a loss, rituals create a sacred space for reflection and connection. They often involve symbolic actions, words, or objects that convey deeper meanings and reinforce community bonds. Participating in or creating personal rituals can imbue everyday life with a sense of reverence and intention, marking the passage of time with meaningful observance.

Nature offers a profound avenue for spiritual exploration, inviting individuals to connect with the beauty and wonder of the natural world. Spending time in nature fosters a sense of awe and gratitude, reminding individuals of their place within the larger ecosystem. Practices such as forest bathing, walking meditations, or simply observing the changing seasons can deepen one's spiritual connection to the earth. Nature serves as both a teacher and a healer, offering lessons in resilience, balance, and interconnectedness.

Acts of service and compassion are central to many spiritual traditions, emphasizing the importance of kindness and generosity. By extending support and care to others, individuals can cultivate a sense of purpose and fulfillment, reinforcing the interconnectedness of all beings. Volunteering, helping a neighbor, or practicing random acts of kindness are ways to embody this spiritual principle in daily life. Such actions not only benefit others but also enrich the giver's spiritual journey, fostering empathy and gratitude.

Exploring spiritual practices is a deeply personal journey, inviting individuals to discover what resonates with their beliefs and values. It is a process of exploration and experimentation, allowing for growth and evolution over time. Each person's spiritual path is unique, shaped by personal experiences, cultural influences, and individual insights. By remaining open to new practices and perspectives, individuals can cultivate a rich and fulfilling spiritual life.

Incorporating spiritual practices into daily life offers a multitude of benefits, enhancing mental, emotional, and physical well-being. These practices provide tools for navigating life's challenges with grace and resilience, fostering a sense of peace and purpose. They encourage individuals to live with intention and authenticity, aligning actions with values and beliefs. Ultimately, spiritual practices invite individuals to embark on a journey of self-discovery and transformation, deepening their connection to themselves, others, and the world around them.

The exploration of spiritual practices is an ongoing adventure, inviting curiosity, compassion, and courage. It is a journey that transcends the boundaries of time and culture, weaving a tapestry of wisdom and insight. By embracing spiritual practices, individuals can unlock the potential for profound growth and healing, nurturing a life of meaning, joy, and connection. Through this journey, the spirit finds its voice, guiding individuals toward a deeper understanding of themselves and the world they inhabit.

The Role of Meditation and Mindfulness

Meditation and mindfulness have emerged as powerful tools in the quest for mental clarity, emotional balance, and personal growth. In the fast-paced modern world, where distractions abound and stress levels are high, these practices offer a refuge—a place to reconnect with oneself and the present moment. They invite individuals to cultivate a sense of awareness and tranquility, fostering a deeper understanding of the mind and its patterns. Exploring the role of meditation and mindfulness reveals their transformative potential for enhancing well-being and enriching daily life.

Meditation, a practice with ancient roots, involves training the mind to focus and redirect thoughts. It can take many forms, from seated meditation with a focus on the breath to walking meditation where attention is given to each step. The primary goal is to achieve a heightened state of awareness and concentration, allowing the practitioner to observe their thoughts and emotions without judgment. This practice can lead to profound insights, helping individuals uncover the underlying causes of stress, anxiety, or dissatisfaction.

Mindfulness, closely related to meditation, is the practice of being fully present and engaged in the current moment. It involves paying attention to thoughts, emotions, and physical sensations with curiosity and openness. Unlike meditation, which is often practiced in structured sessions, mindfulness can be integrated into everyday activities. Whether eating, walking, or working, mindfulness encourages individuals to immerse themselves in the experience, enhancing their connection to the present.

The benefits of meditation and mindfulness are well-documented, with research highlighting their positive impact on mental, emotional, and physical health. Regular practice has been shown to reduce symptoms of stress, anxiety, and depression, promoting a sense of calm and well-being. By fostering emotional regulation, these practices help individuals respond to challenging situations with greater resilience and equanimity. They also enhance cognitive function, improving focus, memory, and decision-making skills.

One of the key mechanisms by which meditation and mindfulness exert their effects is through the cultivation of self-awareness. By observing the mind's activity, practitioners develop an understanding of habitual thought patterns and emotional reactions. This awareness creates space for intentional responses rather than automatic reactions, empowering individuals to make conscious choices aligned with their values and goals. Over time, this practice can lead to lasting changes in behavior and perspective, fostering personal growth and transformation.

Incorporating meditation and mindfulness into daily life requires commitment and practice, but the rewards are well worth the effort. For beginners, starting with short sessions—just a few minutes each day—can build a foundation for a sustainable practice. Finding a quiet space, free from distractions, allows for deeper focus and concentration. Many practitioners find it helpful to use guided meditations, which provide structure and support, especially in the early stages of practice.

As the practice deepens, individuals may choose to experiment with different forms of meditation, exploring techniques that resonate with their personal needs and preferences. Some may find solace in loving-kindness meditation, which involves cultivating compassion and goodwill towards oneself and others. Others may be drawn to body scan meditation, where attention is directed to different parts of the body, promoting relaxation and awareness of physical sensations. Each form of meditation offers unique benefits, allowing for a rich and varied exploration of the mind.

Mindfulness can be seamlessly woven into daily routines, transforming ordinary activities into opportunities for presence and awareness. Simple practices, such as mindful breathing or mindful eating, encourage individuals to slow down and savor each moment. By bringing attention to the sensory experience of eating, for example, individuals can develop a greater appreciation for food, cultivating gratitude and enjoyment. Similarly, mindful breathing provides a quick and accessible way to center oneself amidst the demands of daily life.

The practice of mindfulness extends beyond individual well-being, influencing relationships and interactions with others. By cultivating empathy and compassion, mindfulness enhances communication and fosters deeper connections. It encourages individuals to listen attentively and respond with kindness, nurturing a sense of understanding and mutual respect. In this way, mindfulness contributes to a more harmonious and supportive social environment.

Meditation and mindfulness also offer a valuable framework for navigating the complexities of modern life. In a world filled with constant stimuli and information overload, these practices provide tools for managing attention and maintaining focus. By training the mind to remain present, individuals can reduce the impact of distractions and improve productivity. This heightened awareness also supports creative thinking, allowing for greater innovation and problem-solving.

The journey of meditation and mindfulness is a lifelong exploration, inviting curiosity and openness. It is a path that encourages self-discovery and self-compassion, guiding individuals toward a more authentic and fulfilling life. By embracing these practices, individuals can cultivate a sense of inner peace and resilience, navigating the ebb and flow of life with grace and wisdom.

Meditation and mindfulness are not a panacea, but they offer profound benefits for those willing to engage with the practice. Their transformative potential lies in the ability to reshape the mind and heart, fostering a deeper connection to oneself and the world. As individuals embark on this journey, they discover the power of presence, unlocking the richness and beauty of each moment. Through meditation and mindfulness, the ordinary becomes extraordinary, revealing the limitless possibilities of a life lived with awareness and intention.

Connection with Nature and Its Benefits

In a world dominated by screens and concrete, the connection with nature often feels like a distant memory, a nostalgic echo of simpler times. Yet, the bond humans share with the natural world is intrinsic and profound, woven into the very fabric of existence. Embracing this connection not only enriches lives but also offers numerous physical, mental, and emotional benefits. By rediscovering the joys and tranquility of the natural world, individuals can foster a sense of belonging and well-being that transcends the demands of modern life.

The allure of nature lies in its ability to captivate the senses and rejuvenate the spirit. From the gentle rustle of leaves in the wind to the vibrant colors of a sunset, nature provides a sensory feast that awakens the mind and soothes the soul. This sensory engagement is not merely pleasurable; it also has profound effects on health and happiness. Studies have shown that spending time in nature reduces stress, lowers blood pressure, and boosts mood, offering a natural antidote to the pressures of daily life.

Immersion in natural settings can enhance physical health by encouraging movement and activity. Whether hiking along rugged trails, cycling through lush forests, or strolling along a sandy beach, nature invites exploration and adventure. These activities improve cardiovascular fitness, strengthen muscles, and increase endurance, contributing to overall well-being. The varied terrains and landscapes provide a dynamic workout that engages the body in ways that indoor exercise cannot replicate.

The mental health benefits of connecting with nature are equally compelling. Nature provides a sanctuary for reflection and introspection, offering a respite from the constant barrage of information and stimuli. Time spent outdoors can enhance creativity, improve focus, and sharpen cognitive function. It allows the mind to wander, fostering problem-solving and innovative thinking. For those struggling with anxiety, depression, or burnout, nature serves as a healing balm, offering peace and perspective.

Emotional well-being is deeply intertwined with the natural world. The rhythm of nature—the cycles of day and night, the changing seasons—resonates with the human experience, providing a sense of continuity and stability. The beauty and majesty of natural landscapes inspire awe and gratitude, lifting the spirit and nurturing the soul. This emotional connection can foster a sense of purpose and fulfillment, encouraging individuals to live with greater intention and compassion.

Building a connection with nature begins with small, intentional actions that invite the outdoors into daily life. Simple practices, such as taking a morning walk in a nearby park or tending to a garden, can cultivate a deeper appreciation for the natural world. Observing the intricate details of a flower, listening to the chorus of birdsong, or feeling the warmth of the sun on the skin fosters mindfulness and presence, enriching the experience of each moment.

For those seeking a more immersive connection, outdoor activities such as camping, kayaking, or rock climbing offer opportunities to engage with nature on a deeper level. These adventures challenge the body and mind, building resilience and confidence. They also foster a sense of camaraderie and shared experience, strengthening bonds with family and friends. Such experiences create lasting memories and deepen the appreciation for the beauty and wonder of the natural world.

Nature also offers valuable lessons in balance and interconnectedness. Observing ecosystems at work reveals the delicate interplay of species and habitats, highlighting the importance of harmony and cooperation. This understanding can inspire greater environmental stewardship, motivating individuals to protect and preserve the natural world. By embracing sustainable practices and advocating for conservation efforts, individuals can contribute to the health and vitality of the planet.

The connection with nature is not limited to wilderness settings; it can be nurtured in urban environments as well. City parks, botanical gardens, and green rooftops provide accessible spaces for nature immersion. Urban gardening and community agriculture initiatives invite residents to engage with nature, fostering community ties and promoting food sustainability. Even small acts, such as bringing plants into the home or office, can create a sense of connection and bring nature's benefits indoors.

For children, the connection with nature is particularly vital, shaping their development and well-being. Outdoor play encourages creativity, curiosity, and problem-solving skills, laying the foundation for lifelong learning and exploration. Nature provides an ideal setting for physical activity, promoting health and fitness from a young age. It also fosters a sense of wonder and discovery, instilling a love for the natural world that can inspire future generations to become caretakers of the environment.

The role of technology in modern life often seems at odds with the natural world, yet it can also be a bridge to deeper connection. Apps and online resources provide tools for identifying plants, tracking wildlife, and exploring outdoor trails, enriching the experience of nature. Virtual communities and social media platforms offer opportunities to share experiences and learn from others, fostering a global appreciation for the natural world.

Ultimately, the connection with nature is a deeply personal journey, inviting individuals to explore their relationship with the earth and all its inhabitants. It is a journey that offers renewal and transformation, guiding individuals toward a more balanced and harmonious way of living. By embracing nature's gifts, individuals can cultivate a sense of peace and purpose, enriching their own lives and contributing to a more vibrant and sustainable world.

The call of the wild resonates within each of us, urging us to step outside, breathe deeply, and embrace the beauty and majesty of the natural world. This connection is not merely a luxury; it is a necessity, vital to our health, happiness, and survival. As we reconnect with nature, we rediscover our place within the web of life, finding solace, inspiration, and meaning in the embrace of the earth. Through this connection, we become stewards of the planet, nurturing a legacy of care and respect for future generations to cherish.

Finding Meaning and Purpose

Finding meaning and purpose is a journey that lies at the heart of the human experience, an odyssey that transcends the mundane and reaches into the soul's deepest yearnings. Throughout history, individuals have sought to understand their place in the world and the reasons behind their existence. This quest for meaning is driven by an innate desire to connect with something greater than oneself, to leave a legacy, and to live a life filled with significance and fulfillment.

The search for meaning often begins with introspection and self-discovery. It involves examining one's values, passions, and beliefs, and understanding how they align with personal goals and aspirations. This process is deeply personal and unique to each individual, requiring honesty and courage to confront both strengths and limitations. By identifying what truly matters, individuals can begin to craft a vision for their lives that reflects their authentic selves and resonates with their inner truth.

For some, meaning is found through relationships and connections with others. Building and nurturing bonds with family, friends, and community can provide a profound sense of purpose. These relationships offer support, love, and a shared sense of belonging, enriching life with joy and companionship. Acts of kindness and service to others further deepen this connection, fostering empathy and compassion while contributing to the greater good. Through these interactions, individuals find purpose in being part of something larger than themselves, creating a ripple effect of positivity and change.

Work and career also play a significant role in the pursuit of meaning and purpose. Engaging in work that aligns with personal values and passions can be a source of immense satisfaction and fulfillment. It provides an opportunity to utilize talents and skills in ways that contribute to personal growth and societal impact. However, finding purpose in one's career is not solely about the nature of the work itself but also about how it is approached. Bringing integrity, creativity, and dedication to any endeavor can transform it into a meaningful pursuit, regardless of the field or position.

Spirituality and faith offer another pathway to discovering meaning and purpose. For many, belief in a higher power or spiritual force provides a framework for understanding life's challenges and triumphs. Spiritual practices, rituals, and teachings offer guidance and insight, helping individuals navigate the complexities of existence with grace and wisdom. This spiritual journey fosters a sense of connection to the divine and to the universe, instilling hope and resilience in the face of adversity.

Personal growth and self-improvement are integral to the quest for meaning and purpose. Embracing a lifelong commitment to learning and development encourages individuals to explore new horizons and push beyond their comfort zones. This pursuit of knowledge and experience broadens perspectives and enhances self-awareness, empowering individuals to live more fully and authentically. By setting and achieving personal goals, individuals cultivate a sense of accomplishment and mastery, reinforcing their sense of purpose and direction.

Creativity and self-expression also hold the key to unlocking meaning and purpose. Engaging in artistic endeavors, whether through writing, painting, music, or dance, allows individuals to explore their inner world and communicate their unique vision. Creativity provides an outlet for emotions and ideas, offering a sense of freedom and liberation. It connects individuals to the universal human experience, fostering empathy and understanding across cultural and social boundaries.

Nature and the environment serve as profound sources of inspiration and meaning. The beauty and majesty of the natural world evoke a sense of wonder and gratitude, reminding individuals of their place within the larger tapestry of life. By cultivating a connection with nature, individuals can find solace and renewal, drawing strength and wisdom from the earth's rhythms and cycles. This relationship also inspires environmental stewardship, motivating individuals to protect and preserve the planet for future generations.

The journey of finding meaning and purpose is not without its challenges. It requires resilience and perseverance, as individuals navigate setbacks, uncertainties, and moments of doubt. Embracing these challenges as opportunities for growth and transformation is essential to the process. By maintaining an open mind and heart, individuals can adapt and evolve, discovering new pathways and perspectives that enrich their understanding and experience.

Ultimately, meaning and purpose are not static destinations but dynamic experiences that evolve over time. Life's circumstances, relationships, and priorities shift, inviting individuals to continually reassess and redefine their path. This ongoing journey fosters a sense of curiosity and exploration, encouraging individuals to remain engaged with the world and with themselves. By embracing this fluidity, individuals can live with intention and authenticity, crafting a life that reflects their deepest values and aspirations.

The quest for meaning and purpose is a deeply personal and transformative endeavor, inviting individuals to explore the depths of their existence and the heights of their potential. It is a journey that requires courage, reflection, and action, guiding individuals toward a life of significance and fulfillment. Through this exploration, individuals can transcend the ordinary, unlocking the extraordinary potential within themselves and the world around them. As they find and embrace their purpose, they become beacons of inspiration and change, illuminating the path for others to follow.

Rituals and Traditions That Center Us

Rituals and traditions serve as anchors in the ever-changing currents of life, offering stability, continuity, and a sense of belonging. These practices, often handed down through generations, imbue our lives with meaning and connect us to our heritage, our communities, and our inner selves. By participating in rituals and traditions, individuals can find grounding and centeredness, creating a sense of order and purpose amidst the chaos of modern existence.

Rituals are deliberate actions imbued with symbolic meaning. They can be as simple as a morning routine or as elaborate as a cultural celebration. At their core, rituals are about intention and presence, transforming the ordinary into the extraordinary. They provide a framework for marking significant events, transitions, and milestones, helping individuals navigate the complexities of life with grace and mindfulness.

Traditions, on the other hand, are the collective practices that define a community or culture. They are the shared customs and beliefs that weave individuals into the fabric of their society, offering a sense of identity and continuity. Traditions are often rooted in historical or religious contexts, yet they evolve over time, adapting to the needs and values of each generation. By participating in traditions, individuals honor their past while contributing to the legacy of their community.

One of the most profound aspects of rituals and traditions is their ability to create a sense of connection. They bring people together, fostering bonds of kinship and understanding. Whether through family gatherings, religious ceremonies, or community festivals, these practices unite individuals in shared experiences, reinforcing the social fabric that holds us together. In a world where technology often isolates us, rituals and traditions offer opportunities for genuine human connection and interaction.

Rituals also serve as powerful tools for personal growth and transformation. They provide a space for reflection, introspection, and intention-setting, allowing individuals to align their actions with their values and goals. By engaging in rituals, individuals can cultivate mindfulness and self-awareness, enhancing their understanding of themselves and their place in the world. Rituals can also facilitate healing and release, offering a way to process emotions and experiences, and to let go of what no longer serves us.

Incorporating rituals into daily life can be a simple yet profound way to find centeredness and balance. Morning rituals, such as meditation, journaling, or setting intentions for the day, create a foundation of mindfulness and focus. Evening rituals, like expressing gratitude or reflecting on the day's experiences, provide closure and peace. These practices invite individuals to pause and be present, nurturing a sense of calm and clarity amidst life's demands.

Traditions, too, offer a source of stability and grounding. They mark the passage of time and the rhythm of the seasons, providing a sense of continuity and predictability. Celebrating holidays, anniversaries, and cultural events connects individuals to their heritage and community, reinforcing a sense of belonging and identity. Traditions also offer opportunities for creativity and expression, allowing individuals to adapt and reinterpret practices in ways that resonate with their personal values and experiences.

For those seeking to create new rituals or traditions, the possibilities are boundless. Personal rituals can be crafted to reflect individual beliefs and aspirations, incorporating elements that hold personal significance. Whether lighting a candle to symbolize hope, planting a tree to honor a loved one, or creating art to express emotions, these rituals become meaningful expressions of one's inner journey. Similarly, new traditions can be established within families or communities, celebrating milestones, achievements, or shared values.

Rituals and traditions also offer a way to engage with the natural world, fostering a sense of connection and reverence for the environment. Seasonal rituals, such as solstice celebrations or harvest festivals, honor the cycles of nature and the interdependence of all living things. These practices encourage individuals to live in harmony with the earth, promoting sustainability and environmental stewardship. By aligning with nature's rhythms, individuals can cultivate a sense of balance and harmony in their own lives.

While rituals and traditions provide benefits across cultural and social contexts, their significance is deeply personal. Each individual's experience of these practices is unique, shaped by personal beliefs, values, and experiences. As such, rituals and traditions invite individuals to explore their own relationship with these practices, discovering what resonates with their spirit and enriches their lives.

In a world that often feels fragmented and disconnected, rituals and traditions offer a sense of wholeness and integration. They remind us of the continuity of life, the interconnectedness of all beings, and the enduring power of the human spirit. By embracing these practices, individuals can find centeredness and peace, grounding themselves in a sense of purpose and belonging.

Ultimately, rituals and traditions are not static relics of the past but dynamic expressions of the present. They evolve with us, reflecting the changing landscapes of our lives and the world around us. By participating in these practices, individuals contribute to the living tapestry of human culture, weaving their own threads into the story of humanity. Through rituals and traditions, we find not only our place in the world but also the strength and inspiration to shape the future.

Chapter 4: Creating a Balanced Lifestyle

Time Management for Well-being

Time management is a crucial skill in achieving well-being, as it intertwines with every aspect of life. With the demands of work, family, and personal pursuits, it often feels like there are never enough hours in the day. However, effective time management is not about squeezing more tasks into an already packed schedule but about prioritizing and organizing time to align with personal values and goals. By mastering this skill, individuals can reduce stress, enhance productivity, and create space for activities that nourish the body, mind, and spirit.

The first step in effective time management is understanding where time is currently spent. This involves tracking daily activities to identify patterns, habits, and potential time-wasters. Many people are surprised to discover how much time is consumed by unproductive activities such as excessive screen time or unnecessary multitasking. By gaining insight into these habits, individuals can make informed decisions about how to allocate their time more intentionally.

Once time usage is understood, setting clear and realistic goals becomes essential. These goals should reflect both short-term tasks and long-term aspirations, serving as a guide for daily decision-making. By breaking goals into manageable steps, individuals can create a roadmap for success while avoiding the overwhelm that often accompanies larger projects. Prioritization is key, ensuring that time and energy are focused on activities that align with personal values and contribute to overall well-being.

Creating a structured schedule is a powerful tool for managing time effectively. This schedule should include blocks of time dedicated to specific tasks, allowing for focused attention and minimizing distractions. It is important to build in flexibility, recognizing that unexpected events may arise. By allowing for adjustments and maintaining a mindset of adaptability, individuals can navigate changes without losing sight of their priorities.

An often-overlooked aspect of time management is the importance of rest and rejuvenation. Scheduling breaks and downtime is crucial for maintaining energy and focus throughout the day. Short breaks can refresh the mind and body, enhancing productivity and creativity. Additionally, prioritizing quality sleep is fundamental to well-being, affecting mood, cognitive function, and overall health. By valuing rest as an integral part of time management, individuals can prevent burnout and sustain high levels of performance.

Delegation is another effective strategy for time management. Many individuals feel compelled to take on every responsibility themselves, leading to stress and inefficiency. By identifying tasks that can be shared or outsourced, individuals can free up time for activities that align more closely with their strengths and priorities. This not only enhances personal productivity but also fosters collaboration and teamwork, strengthening relationships with colleagues, family, and friends.

Mindfulness and presence play a significant role in managing time for well-being. By focusing attention on the present moment, individuals can complete tasks more efficiently and with greater satisfaction. Mindfulness reduces the tendency to rush through activities or become distracted, allowing for a deeper engagement with each task. This practice can be incorporated into daily routines, whether through mindful breathing during work or savoring each bite during meals.

Technology offers both opportunities and challenges in the realm of time management. While digital tools and apps can assist in organizing tasks and reminders, they also pose the risk of distraction and information overload. It is important to use technology mindfully, setting boundaries and limits to ensure it serves rather than detracts from time management goals. By harnessing the benefits of technology while minimizing its drawbacks, individuals can enhance their ability to manage time effectively.

Balancing various aspects of life is a dynamic process, requiring ongoing reflection and adjustment. Regularly reviewing and reassessing priorities allows individuals to make informed choices about how to allocate time and energy. This process involves recognizing when certain activities or commitments no longer serve one's well-being and making necessary changes. By remaining open to growth and change, individuals can maintain a sense of balance and harmony in their lives.

Embracing the concept of "time abundance" can transform the way individuals approach time management. This mindset shift involves recognizing that there is enough time to focus on what truly matters, rather than feeling constantly rushed or pressured. By letting go of the need to do everything and instead focusing on quality over quantity, individuals can find greater satisfaction and fulfillment in their daily lives.

Ultimately, effective time management is not about rigid control but about creating a life that reflects one's values and aspirations. It is a journey of self-discovery and empowerment, inviting individuals to take ownership of their time and their choices. By aligning time management practices with personal well-being, individuals can cultivate a life that is both productive and meaningful, nurturing body, mind, and spirit.

In this journey, patience and self-compassion are essential. There will be days when plans go awry and schedules fall apart, but these moments offer valuable lessons and opportunities for growth. By approaching time management with curiosity and flexibility, individuals can adapt and evolve, discovering new strategies and insights along the way.

Time is a precious and finite resource, but with mindful management, it can be a source of joy, creativity, and fulfillment. By embracing time management as a tool for well-being, individuals can enhance their quality of life, finding balance and harmony in a world that often feels hurried and chaotic. Through this practice, they can create a life that reflects their deepest values and aspirations, leaving a legacy of presence and purpose.

Prioritizing Self-Care

Self-care often finds itself relegated to the bottom of a never-ending to-do list, overshadowed by the demands of work, family, and social commitments. Yet, it is the cornerstone of well-being, providing the foundation upon which a balanced and fulfilling life is built. Prioritizing self-care is not an indulgence; it is a necessity that enables individuals to perform at their best, maintain resilience in the face of challenges, and lead a life enriched with joy and contentment.

The concept of self-care encompasses a broad range of activities and practices that nurture the body, mind, and spirit. It is deeply personal, varying from person to person, and evolves with changing needs and circumstances. At its core, self-care involves recognizing one's own worth and making a conscious decision to honor and care for oneself. This commitment to self-nurturance is both empowering and transformative, creating a ripple effect that enhances all areas of life.

Physical self-care forms the foundation of well-being, addressing the body's needs for nourishment, movement, and rest. A balanced diet rich in nutrients fuels the body and mind, providing the energy needed to tackle daily tasks and challenges. Regular physical activity, whether through yoga, jogging, or dancing, strengthens the body, releases endorphins, and boosts mood. Equally important is the need for restorative sleep, which allows the body to heal and rejuvenate, supporting optimal health and vitality.

Mental self-care involves nurturing the mind and cultivating a positive and resilient mindset. This can be achieved through practices such as mindfulness, meditation, and journaling, which promote clarity, focus, and emotional balance. Engaging in activities that stimulate the mind, such as reading, puzzles, or learning a new skill, keeps the brain active and engaged. Setting healthy boundaries and learning to say no are also essential components of mental self-care, protecting one's time and energy from unnecessary stress and overwhelm.

Emotional self-care requires acknowledging and honoring one's feelings, allowing for the full expression of emotions without judgment or suppression. This can involve seeking support from friends, family, or mental health professionals, as well as engaging in creative outlets such as art, music, or writing. Practicing self-compassion and forgiveness fosters emotional resilience, enabling individuals to navigate life's ups and downs with grace and acceptance.

Spiritual self-care, though often overlooked, is equally important in nurturing a sense of purpose and connection. This does not necessarily involve religious practices, but rather activities that align with one's values and beliefs, fostering a sense of meaning and fulfillment. This could include spending time in nature, practicing gratitude, or engaging in meditation or prayer. By cultivating a connection with something greater than oneself, individuals can find solace and inspiration, grounding themselves in the present moment.

Creating a self-care plan that reflects individual needs and preferences is an essential step in prioritizing self-care. This plan should include a mix of daily, weekly, and monthly activities that address various aspects of well-being. Flexibility is key, allowing for adjustments as circumstances change. It is important to remember that self-care is not a one-size-fits-all approach, and what works for one person may not work for another. The goal is to create a plan that feels nurturing and sustainable, supporting overall health and happiness.

Incorporating self-care into daily routines can be achieved through small, intentional actions that build over time. This could involve starting the day with a few moments of meditation, taking a walk during lunch breaks, or setting aside time for hobbies and relaxation in the evening. By integrating self-care into daily life, individuals can create a sense of balance and stability, reducing stress and enhancing well-being.

It is important to recognize that self-care is not a solitary endeavor but can be enriched through connection with others. Sharing self-care activities with friends, family, or community groups can foster a sense of belonging and support, enhancing the overall experience. Collaborative activities such as group exercise classes, cooking together, or participating in volunteer work can strengthen relationships and create a sense of camaraderie and shared purpose.

Overcoming barriers to self-care is a common challenge, as individuals often feel guilty or selfish for prioritizing their own needs. It is essential to reframe self-care as an act of self-respect and responsibility, recognizing that caring for oneself enables individuals to care for others more effectively. By letting go of guilt and embracing the importance of self-care, individuals can create a positive cycle of well-being that benefits both themselves and those around them.

Self-care also involves being attuned to one's body and mind, recognizing signs of stress, fatigue, or imbalance. By listening to these signals and responding with compassion and care, individuals can prevent burnout and maintain a state of equilibrium. This requires a commitment to self-awareness and ongoing reflection, allowing for adjustments and recalibration as needed.

Ultimately, prioritizing self-care is a journey of self-discovery and empowerment, inviting individuals to explore what truly nourishes and sustains them. It is an ongoing process that evolves with time, requiring patience, flexibility, and dedication.

By embracing self-care as an integral part of life, individuals can cultivate a sense of joy, resilience, and fulfillment, creating a life that reflects their deepest values and aspirations.

Through this commitment to self-care, individuals can transform their relationship with themselves and the world around them, fostering a sense of balance and harmony that enriches every aspect of their lives. By prioritizing self-care, they lay the foundation for a life filled with vitality, purpose, and well-being, nurturing body, mind, and spirit in the process.

Building Routines for Balance

Routines serve as the silent architects of our daily lives, shaping the rhythm and flow of our activities. They provide structure and predictability, offering a sense of stability in an otherwise chaotic world. Building routines that foster balance is an art that requires intention, reflection, and adaptability. When crafted thoughtfully, routines can enhance well-being, productivity, and overall life satisfaction, creating a harmonious blend of work, leisure, and self-care.

The journey of building effective routines begins with self-awareness. Understanding one's natural tendencies, energy levels, and preferences provides insight into how best to structure daily activities. Some people thrive in the early morning, while others find their stride in the afternoon or evening. By aligning routines with these natural rhythms, individuals can optimize their energy and focus, making the most of each moment.

One of the key elements of a balanced routine is prioritization. Identifying core values and goals helps individuals determine what truly matters, guiding the allocation of time and resources. This process involves distinguishing between tasks that are essential and those that are optional, ensuring that time is spent on activities that contribute to personal growth and fulfillment. By focusing on what is most important, individuals can create routines that reflect their aspirations and support their well-being.

Morning routines set the tone for the day, providing a foundation of calm and clarity. Simple practices such as stretching, meditation, or a nourishing breakfast can ground individuals, preparing them for the challenges ahead. These rituals create a sense of intentionality, allowing individuals to approach the day with a positive mindset and focused energy. The key is to keep morning routines manageable and enjoyable, avoiding the temptation to over-schedule or rush through them.

Work routines play a crucial role in maintaining balance, particularly in a world where the lines between work and personal life often blur. Establishing clear boundaries and designated workspaces helps create a sense of separation, allowing individuals to focus fully on work tasks without unnecessary distractions. Time-blocking techniques can enhance productivity, allocating specific periods for focused work, meetings, and breaks. Regular breaks are essential, providing opportunities to recharge and reset, ultimately boosting creativity and efficiency.

Evening routines offer a chance to unwind and reflect, transitioning from the demands of the day to a state of relaxation and rest. Activities such as reading, journaling, or spending time with loved ones can provide a sense of closure, allowing individuals to release the day's stresses and prepare for restorative sleep. Limiting screen time and creating a calming environment further supports this transition, promoting a peaceful end to the day.

Flexibility is a vital component of any balanced routine. Life is inherently unpredictable, and routines must be adaptable to accommodate changing circumstances. This flexibility involves recognizing when routines need adjustment and allowing for spontaneity and creativity. By embracing change and remaining open to new possibilities, individuals can maintain a sense of balance even amidst life's uncertainties.

Building routines for balance is not a solitary endeavor but can be enriched through collaboration with others. Involving family members, friends, or colleagues in the process creates a sense of shared purpose and support, enhancing the overall experience. Collaborative routines, such as family meals or team check-ins, strengthen relationships and foster a sense of community and connection.

Overcoming obstacles to routine-building is a common challenge, as individuals often struggle with consistency or motivation. The key is to start small, focusing on one or two habits at a time, and gradually building upon them. Celebrating small successes and progress reinforces positive behavior, creating momentum and motivation to continue. It is also important to practice self-compassion, recognizing that setbacks are a natural part of the process and an opportunity for growth and learning.

Technology can be both a friend and foe in the quest for balanced routines. While digital tools and apps offer convenience and organization, they can also contribute to distraction and overwhelm. Mindful use of technology involves setting boundaries, such as designated screen-free times or app limits, to ensure it serves rather than hinders routine-building efforts. By harnessing the benefits of technology while minimizing its drawbacks, individuals can enhance their ability to create and maintain balanced routines.

The process of building routines for balance is a dynamic and ongoing journey, requiring regular reflection and reassessment. Periodically reviewing routines allows individuals to make informed adjustments, ensuring they continue to meet evolving needs and goals. This process involves recognizing when certain habits or activities no longer serve one's well-being and making necessary changes. By remaining open to growth and change, individuals can maintain a sense of balance and harmony in their lives.

Ultimately, building routines for balance is about creating a life that reflects one's values and aspirations. It is a journey of self-discovery and empowerment, inviting individuals to take ownership of their time and choices. By aligning routines with personal well-being, individuals can cultivate a life that is both productive and meaningful, nurturing body, mind, and spirit.

Through this commitment to balanced routines, individuals can transform their relationship with time and create a sense of stability and fulfillment. By prioritizing balance, they lay the foundation for a life filled with vitality, purpose, and well-being, nurturing all aspects of their being in the process.

The Art of Saying No

Saying "no" is a skill that many struggle to master, yet it holds the key to personal freedom and empowerment. In a world overflowing with demands and expectations, knowing when and how to say "no" can transform one's life, creating space for what truly matters. The art of saying "no" is not about rejection or negativity; it is about setting boundaries, protecting one's time and energy, and aligning actions with values and priorities.

For many, the difficulty in saying "no" stems from a desire to please others and avoid conflict. This tendency often leads to overcommitment, stress, and resentment, as individuals find themselves stretched thin, trying to meet everyone else's needs. The first step in mastering the art of saying "no" is shifting the mindset from one of obligation to one of choice. Recognizing that every "yes" is a commitment of time and energy allows individuals to weigh decisions more carefully, considering whether they align with personal goals and values.

Understanding one's priorities is essential in making informed decisions about when to say "no." By clarifying what truly matters, individuals can create a framework for evaluating requests and opportunities. This involves distinguishing between activities that contribute to personal growth and well-being and those that detract from them. By focusing on what is most important, individuals can confidently decline requests that do not serve their best interests.

Saying "no" effectively requires clear and honest communication. It is important to be direct and respectful, expressing gratitude for the opportunity or invitation while clearly stating one's decision. Offering a brief explanation, if appropriate, can provide context and understanding, although it is not always necessary. The key is to deliver the message with confidence and kindness, maintaining positive relationships while asserting one's boundaries.

Practicing assertiveness is a valuable skill in saying "no." This involves expressing one's needs and desires firmly and respectfully, without apologizing or justifying the decision excessively. Assertiveness empowers individuals to take ownership of their choices, fostering self-respect and self-confidence. It also sets a precedent for how one expects to be treated, encouraging others to respect one's boundaries.

Anticipating and managing potential reactions is an important aspect of saying "no." Some individuals may respond with disappointment or pressure, attempting to persuade or guilt one into changing their decision. It is crucial to remain steadfast and composed, reiterating one's decision if necessary and avoiding the temptation to waver or compromise. By standing firm, individuals reinforce their boundaries and demonstrate commitment to their values.

Saying "no" is not solely about turning down requests from others but also involves setting limits with oneself. This includes recognizing when to step back from obligations or activities that no longer serve one's well-being. It may involve saying "no" to perfectionism, overworking, or unhealthy habits, creating space for rest, relaxation, and self-care. By setting boundaries with oneself, individuals can cultivate a more balanced and fulfilling life.

The art of saying "no" extends to technology and media consumption, where boundaries are often blurred. In a digital age where constant connectivity is the norm, setting limits on screen time and information intake is crucial for mental and emotional well-being. This involves saying "no" to unnecessary notifications, mindless scrolling, or excessive multitasking, creating space for focused and intentional engagement with the world.

Building a supportive network can enhance one's ability to say "no" effectively. Surrounding oneself with individuals who respect and understand one's boundaries fosters a sense of community and encouragement. Sharing experiences and strategies with others can provide valuable insights and reinforce the importance of setting limits. By fostering supportive relationships, individuals can create an environment where saying "no" is respected and valued.

Overcoming guilt and fear is a common challenge in the art of saying "no." Many individuals feel guilty for prioritizing their own needs or fear the potential consequences of declining requests. It is important to remember that saying "no" is an act of self-care and empowerment, allowing individuals to focus on what truly matters. By reframing "no" as a positive choice, individuals can release guilt and embrace the freedom that comes with setting boundaries.

The journey of mastering the art of saying "no" is a process of self-discovery and growth. It involves ongoing reflection and practice, as individuals learn to navigate the complexities of relationships and commitments. By remaining open to growth and change, individuals can refine their ability to set boundaries, creating a life that reflects their values and aspirations.

Ultimately, the art of saying "no" is about creating a life that is authentic and fulfilling. It is a journey of empowerment, inviting individuals to take ownership of their time and choices. By aligning actions with personal well-being, individuals can cultivate a life that is both productive and meaningful, nurturing body, mind, and spirit.

Through this commitment to saying "no," individuals can transform their relationship with themselves and the world around them, fostering a sense of balance and harmony that enriches every aspect of their lives. By prioritizing boundaries, they lay the foundation for a life filled with vitality, purpose, and well-being, nurturing all aspects of their being in the process.

Harmonizing Work and Personal Life

Balancing the demands of work and personal life is a challenge faced by many in today's fast-paced world. The quest for harmony between professional responsibilities and personal well-being can often feel elusive, with the scales tipping too far in one direction at the expense of the other. Achieving this balance requires intention, flexibility, and a commitment to aligning one's life with core values and priorities.

A crucial step in harmonizing work and personal life is understanding what truly matters. This involves identifying personal values and setting clear goals that reflect both professional aspirations and personal desires. By clarifying these priorities, individuals can create a framework for making decisions about how to spend their time and energy. This process involves distinguishing between what is essential and what is negotiable, ensuring that actions align with long-term goals and contribute to overall life satisfaction.

Time management plays a pivotal role in achieving harmony between work and personal life. Effective time management involves more than just organizing tasks; it's about creating a schedule that reflects one's values and priorities. This includes setting boundaries to protect personal time and ensuring that work commitments do not encroach upon it. By allocating specific times for work, family, leisure, and self-care, individuals can create a balanced routine that nurtures all aspects of their life.

Setting boundaries is essential in maintaining a healthy work-life balance. This involves defining clear lines between work and personal time, both physically and mentally. For those working from home, creating a designated workspace can help establish this separation, allowing individuals to switch between work and personal modes more easily. Communicating these boundaries to colleagues and family members ensures mutual understanding and respect, reducing the likelihood of conflict and stress.

Flexibility is a key component in harmonizing work and personal life. Life is inherently unpredictable, and the ability to adapt to changing circumstances is crucial in maintaining balance. This means being open to adjusting schedules and priorities as needed, while still keeping long-term goals in sight. Embracing change and cultivating resilience allows individuals to navigate challenges with grace and maintain a sense of equilibrium even amidst uncertainty.

Incorporating self-care into daily routines is vital for sustaining energy and well-being. This involves setting aside time for activities that nourish the body, mind, and spirit, such as exercise, meditation, or creative pursuits. By prioritizing self-care, individuals can enhance their resilience and capacity to manage stress, ultimately supporting their ability to balance work and personal life. Self-care is not a luxury, but a necessity that enables individuals to perform at their best in all areas of life.

The role of technology in the quest for work-life balance cannot be overlooked. While technology offers convenience and connectivity, it also poses the risk of blurring boundaries and contributing to burnout. Setting limits on screen time and establishing tech-free zones or times can help mitigate these risks, allowing individuals to be fully present in their personal lives. By using technology mindfully, individuals can harness its benefits while minimizing its drawbacks, supporting a more balanced lifestyle.

Creating a supportive environment is essential in harmonizing work and personal life. This involves building a network of understanding and supportive individuals, both at work and at home. Sharing responsibilities with partners, family members, or colleagues can lighten the load and foster a sense of teamwork and collaboration. Engaging in open communication and expressing needs and desires can strengthen relationships and create a more supportive atmosphere.

Work-life balance is not a static state but a dynamic process that requires ongoing reflection and adjustment. Regularly reassessing priorities and routines allows individuals to make informed decisions about how to allocate their time and energy. This process involves recognizing when certain commitments or activities no longer serve one's well-being and making necessary changes. By remaining open to growth and change, individuals can maintain a sense of balance and harmony in their lives.

Embracing the concept of integration rather than separation can transform the way individuals approach work-life balance.

This mindset involves viewing work and personal life as interconnected and complementary, rather than as competing forces. By finding ways to integrate personal values and passions into professional pursuits, individuals can create a more fulfilling and harmonious life. This may involve pursuing work that aligns with personal interests or finding ways to incorporate family and leisure activities into the workday.

Ultimately, harmonizing work and personal life is about creating a life that reflects one's values and aspirations. It is a journey of self-discovery and empowerment, inviting individuals to take ownership of their time and choices. By aligning work and personal life with personal well-being, individuals can cultivate a life that is both productive and meaningful, nurturing body, mind, and spirit.

Through this commitment to balance, individuals can transform their relationship with work and personal life, fostering a sense of stability and fulfillment. By prioritizing harmony, they lay the foundation for a life filled with vitality, purpose, and well-being, nurturing all aspects of their being in the process.

Chapter 5: Holistic Nutrition and Healing1

Understanding the Role of Nutrition in Wellness

Nutrition is a fundamental pillar of wellness, intricately linked to every aspect of health and well-being. The foods we consume provide the essential nutrients our bodies need to function optimally, influencing physical health, mental clarity, emotional balance, and overall vitality. Understanding the role of nutrition in wellness is not just about dietary choices but about cultivating a deeper connection with the sources of nourishment, recognizing how food impacts every facet of life, and making conscious decisions that support personal well-being.

The journey toward nutritional wellness begins with knowledge—understanding the basic components of a healthy diet and how they contribute to bodily functions. Macronutrients—carbohydrates, proteins, and fats—serve as the body's primary energy sources, each playing distinct and critical roles. Carbohydrates, found in foods like grains, fruits, and vegetables, are the body's preferred energy source, fueling both physical activity and mental processes. Proteins, composed of amino acids, are vital for building and repairing tissues and supporting immune function. Healthy fats, such as those found in nuts, seeds, and avocados, are essential for brain health, hormone production, and cell integrity.

Equally important are micronutrients—vitamins and minerals—that, though required in smaller quantities, are indispensable for maintaining health. Vitamins such as A, C, and E act as antioxidants, protecting the body from oxidative stress, while minerals like calcium and magnesium are crucial for bone health and muscle function. A varied and balanced diet, rich in colorful fruits and vegetables, whole grains, lean proteins, and healthy fats, ensures an adequate intake of these essential nutrients, supporting overall wellness.

Beyond macronutrients and micronutrients, the role of hydration in wellness cannot be overstated. Water is the cornerstone of life, facilitating digestion, nutrient absorption, and waste elimination. Adequate hydration supports cognitive function, regulates body temperature, and maintains healthy skin. Listening to the body's thirst cues and aiming for consistent fluid intake throughout the day can help prevent dehydration and its associated impacts on health and well-being.

The relationship between nutrition and mental health is an area of growing interest and research. Emerging evidence suggests that dietary patterns can influence mood, cognitive function, and emotional resilience. Diets rich in whole foods, such as the Mediterranean diet, which emphasizes fruits, vegetables, whole grains, and healthy fats, have been associated with lower rates of depression and anxiety. Conversely, diets high in processed foods, sugars, and unhealthy fats may exacerbate mood disorders and cognitive decline. By prioritizing nutrient-dense foods, individuals can support not only physical health but also mental and emotional well-being.

Understanding the role of nutrition in wellness also involves recognizing the impact of dietary habits on long-term health outcomes. Chronic diseases such as heart disease, diabetes, and certain cancers have been linked to poor dietary choices, including high consumption of processed foods, sugars, and unhealthy fats. By adopting a diet rich in whole foods and minimizing processed foods, individuals can reduce the risk of these diseases, promoting longevity and quality of life.

Incorporating mindful eating practices can enhance the connection between nutrition and wellness. Mindful eating involves paying attention to the sensory experience of eating, such as the taste, texture, and aroma of food, as well as recognizing hunger and fullness cues. This practice encourages a more conscious and intentional approach to eating, reducing the likelihood of overeating and fostering a healthier relationship with food. By savoring each bite and appreciating the nourishment food provides, individuals can cultivate a deeper sense of gratitude and satisfaction.

The role of nutrition in wellness is also influenced by cultural and personal preferences, acknowledging that dietary choices are deeply personal and often rooted in tradition and identity. Embracing cultural diversity in dietary practices can enrich the understanding of nutrition, offering a variety of flavors, ingredients, and preparation methods that contribute to overall well-being. By exploring and celebrating diverse culinary traditions, individuals can expand their nutritional repertoire and discover new ways to nourish body and soul.

Practical strategies for enhancing nutritional wellness involve planning and preparation. Meal planning, grocery shopping with a list, and preparing meals at home can help ensure that nutritious options are readily available and reduce reliance on convenience foods. Batch cooking and using leftovers creatively can save time and effort while promoting balanced eating throughout the week. By establishing routines and habits that support nutritious choices, individuals can create a sustainable approach to nutrition that fits their lifestyle and goals.

Navigating the abundance of nutritional information available today can be overwhelming, with conflicting advice and fad diets often complicating the path to wellness. It is important to approach nutrition with a critical eye, seeking guidance from credible sources such as registered dietitians or nutrition experts. By focusing on evidence-based practices and individualized approaches, individuals can make informed decisions about their dietary choices, supporting both immediate and long-term health.

Ultimately, understanding the role of nutrition in wellness is about embracing a holistic perspective on health, recognizing that what we eat profoundly impacts how we feel, function, and thrive. It is a journey of exploration and empowerment, inviting individuals to take ownership of their nutritional choices and cultivate a life that reflects their values and aspirations. By aligning dietary practices with personal well-being, individuals can create a foundation for a life filled with vitality, purpose, and joy, nourishing body, mind, and spirit in harmony.

www.ingramcontent.com/pod-product-compliance
Lightning Source LLC
Chambersburg PA
CBHW071226130726
47998CB00002B/847